09655209

Confronting female genita

Through the voices of the peoples of Africa and the global South, Pambazuka Press and Pambazuka News disseminate analysis and debate on the struggle for freedom and justice.

## Pambazuka Press

www.pambazukapress.org

A Pan-African publisher of progressive books and DVDs on Africa and the global South that aim to stimulate discussion, analysis and engagement. Our publications address issues of human rights, social justice, advocacy, the politics of aid, development and international finance, women's rights, emerging powers and activism. They are primarily written by well-known African academics and activists. Most books are also available as ebooks.

## Pambazuka News

www.pambazuka.org

The award-winning and influential electronic weekly newsletter providing a platform for progressive Pan-African perspectives on politics, development and global affairs. With more than 2,500 contributors across the continent and a readership of more than 660,000, Pambazuka News has become the indispensable source of authentic voices of Africa's social analysts and activists.

## Pambazuka Press and Pambazuka News

are published by Fahamu (www.fahamu.org)

# Confronting female genital mutilation

The role of youth and ICTs in changing Africa

**Marie-Hélène Mottin-Sylla and Joëlle Palmieri**

Translated by Mamsaït Jagne

Pambazuka
Press

**enda third world**

**International Development Research Centre**
Ottawa • Cairo • Dakar • Montevideo • Nairobi • New Delhi • Singapore

Published 2011 by Pambazuka Press, the International Development
Research Centre and Environnement et Développement du Tiers Monde

Pambazuka Press, an imprint of Fahamu
Cape Town, Dakar, Nairobi and Oxford
www.pambazukapress.org   www.fahamubooks.org   www.pambazuka.org

Fahamu, 2nd floor, 51 Cornmarket Street, Oxford OX1 3HA, UK
Fahamu Kenya, PO Box 47158, 00100 GPO, Nairobi, Kenya
Fahamu Senegal, 9 Cité Sonatel 2, BP 13083 Dakar Grand-Yoff, Dakar,
Senegal
Fahamu South Africa, c/o 19 Nerina Crescent, Fish Hoek, 7975 Cape Town,
South Africa

International Development Research Centre
PO Box 8500, Ottawa, ON K1G 3H9, Canada
www.idrc.ca / info@idrc.ca

Environnement et Développement du Tiers Monde, BP 3370, Dakar, Senegal

© ENDA 2011

British Library Cataloguing in Publication Data
A catalogue record for this book is available from the British Library

ISBN   978-0-85749-031-5 paperback (Pambazuka Press)
ISBN   978-1-55250-518-2 e-book (IDRC)

Manufactured in the UK by Printondemand-worldwide.com

# Contents

# Drawing boards and boxes

# Abbreviations and acronyms

| | |
|---|---|
| AIDOS | Associazione Italiana Donne per lo Sviluppo |
| ARH | Adolescent reproductive health |
| BF | Burkina Faso |
| CBO | Community-based organisation |
| ECA | Economic Commission for Africa |
| ENDA | Environmental Development Action in the Third World |
| FAWE | Forum of African Women Educationalists |
| FGM | Female genital mutilation |
| FLE | Family life education |
| GEEP | Groupe pour l'Étude et l'Enseignement de la Population |
| IAC | Inter-African Committee on Traditional Practices Affecting the Health of Women and Children |
| ICT–FGM | 'Contribution of ICTs to the Abandonment of FGM in Francophone West Africa: The Citizenship Role of Youth' (Project) |
| ICTs | Information and communications technologies |
| IDRC | International Development Research Centre |
| IEC | Information, education, communication |
| ML | Mali |
| NGO | Non-governmental organisation |
| RH | Reproductive health |
| SN | Senegal |
| UNICEF | United Nations Children's Fund |
| WARF | West Africa Rural Foundation |
| WSIS | World Summit on the Information Society |

# Acknowledgements

First, we would like to thank the communities of Bobo-Dioulasso (Burkina-Faso), Ségou (Mali) and Tambacounda (Senegal), as well as the youth associations of these communities that participated in the ICT–FGM project: Mousso Dambe association in Bobo-Dioulasso, Nietàa association in Ségou and the FLE Clubs of the GEEP regional centre in Tambacounda.

We would also like to express our feelings of friendship and gratitude to the young girls and boys and adults who partici-pated, organised and enriched the project activities, particularly Manhamoudou Ouedraogo and Wassa Traore in Burkina-Faso; Mariam Cheikh Kamate and Youssouf Maïga in Mali; and Fa-toumata Bathily and Richard Biesse in Senegal, who took part in the evaluation of the ICT–FGM project, as well as the resource persons and those who participated in the virtual forum of the project.

This publication owes much to the researchers, coaches and consultants involved in the project: Maria Bicaba Traore, Haoua Kone Tago, Wendkouni Fanta Kouraogo, Ousmane Traore and Toussaint Sankara in Burkina-Faso; Safiatou Coulibaly Malet, Lanceny Diallo, Mohamed Baba and Demba Doucoure in Mali; Foula Ba, Jacqueline Cabral, Mamadou Guène, Mbaye Babacar Gueye, Augustin Ndecky and Papa Ibrahima Thiam in Senegal; Seynabou Badiane, Mor Mbaye Ndiaye, Thiendou Niang, Issa Saka, Molly Melching, Joëlle Palmieri and Fatimata Seye Sylla for their intellectual contribution and social commitment during the implementation of the project. We wish to express our gratitude to them as well as to all the members of the scientific committee: Daniel Annerose (Manobi), Nafissatou Diop (Population Council); Abdou Fall (WARF); Morissanda Kouyate (IAC); Momar Lo (Réseau des Parlementaires du Sahel Population et Développement); Laurence Maréchal (FAWE); Khadidiatou Thiam and Jamylatou Thiam (GEEP); Maria Gabriella De Vita and Lalla Touré (UNICEF), who supervised the project implementation.

On behalf of ENDA and ICT–FGM project partners, I wish to thank the IDRC through Ramata Molo Thioune, Principal Director of Programmes at the Regional Office for West and Central Africa (WARO, Dakar, Senegal).

*Marie-Hélène Mottin-Sylla, ENDA*
*ICT–FGM Project Coordinator*

# Foreword

By making ICTs and the contribution of youth central to all the efforts and strategies aimed at eradicating FGM in francophone West Africa, ENDA shows that it is determined to effect a clean break, which should be taken at face value.

The first challenge regarding FGM was how to talk about it: to name the nameless, speak the unspeakable, make sense out of something that makes no sense so far as human rights and dignity are concerned. By giving black women the opportunity to speak for themselves three decades ago, Awa Thiam let out of the bag what was considered private and taboo, an ancient practice sanctioned by tradition and culture. That breach was further widened by the struggle of many women and human rights activists. By using legal and medical language and making it women's business, this struggle unwittingly imposed on itself limitations in the form of cognitive, cultural, methodological and strategic biases that were bound to compromise the achievement of its main goal.

The merit of ENDA's approach is undoubtedly the highlighting of three essential types of deconstruction, which

- ascribe FGM to a single gender – while women physically endure FGM, they are not the only actors involved;
- confine the practice to a strictly private domain – it is an issue that concerns society in its political dimension;
- connects it directly with a land, tradition and culture.

To show that FGM is a social and political issue, and therefore concerns both men and women as members of the human community, is tantamount to saying that it can only be stopped by the adoption of a holistic approach. The world of that human community is no longer a land whose boundaries are delineated by a memory that lends meaning and legitimacy to customs and traditions that must be preserved as part of a cultural heritage, but rather a global village whose symbols and values are in free circulation, thanks in no small measure to information and communications technologies.

These values should serve the purpose of reconnecting with a dignified humanity by reviving that ancient but still relevant imperative that Kant expressed when he wrote that 'other people should be considered not as a means but as an end'. Hence, stopping FGM is less a matter of engaging a memory, history or culture than having a vision, a future to build with deeply humanistic values. It is obviously necessary to try to put a stop to such practices, but beyond that the real task is to try to construct a tradition that is worthy of being passed on. In that sense, Souleymane Bachir Diagne rightly sees in tradition not the values that are deposited, but the evaluations and re-evaluations of those values.

A precondition to constructing such a genuinely humanistic tradition is respect for human dignity, which is inconceivable without respect for its primary locus: the human body, and more significantly the body of a woman, which is considered sacred because it bears life. This vision, this tradition, naturally includes youth, because they are the recipients and custodians of this legacy. It is with them that we should build the future world, which is no longer ours but most definitely theirs. They live in this world by being connected, by constantly moving to and fro between the real and the virtual, between the local and the global. Is not this token of their times the most beautiful way to show that, in every corner of our planet, the practice of FGM is finally being abandoned?

*Aminata Diaw*
*Senior Lecturer, Department of Philosophy*
*Cheikh Anta Diop University, Dakar*

# Introduction

The African information society is developing very fast. Information and communications technologies (ICTs) are no longer a novelty. Daily life has changed completely, and many certainties and practices have been modified, especially for youth. One might therefore wonder whether it would be relevant to look at the consequences this could have, in Africa and elsewhere, on how female circumcision is perceived, considered and addressed.

But how is the subject to be examined? The study described in this volume reached the conclusion that in the era of the Internet the abandonment of female genital mutilation (FGM)[1] in Africa is primarily a question of youth, gender and citizenship, which imposes a cross-cutting vision of development. Thus, this work sets out to convey the conviction that putting youth and gender at the centre of development issues, in the era of ICTs, helps speed up the citizenry's abandonment of FGM.

The book is intended for a scientific and academic readership, researchers specialising in the social sciences and working on issues related to development – gender and development, youth in development, FGM, ICTs and development, citizenship. On the basis of the research findings and recommendations of the ICT–FGM project, the volume shows why it is important to take into account the impacts of the sudden emergence of the African information society on policy. In this regard, it is also expected to engage decision-makers, heads of institutions, parliamentarians and development project managers on the need to decompartmentalise the conventionally fragmented visions of development so that, in view of the penetration of ICTs in francophone West Africa, youth and gender can be placed at the centre of civic and democratic processes.

## 25 years for the abandonment of FGM

What has been the impact of 25 years[2] of coordinated interventions, strategies and policies implemented on the issue of FGM in the world and in Africa, particularly in francophone West Africa? How and by whom has the issue of FGM been addressed? What have been the resultant initiatives and interventions, in terms of policies, strategies and in the field? In what circles: international, regional, sub-regional, national, local, village, community, family, private? Who have been the protagonists, active, and the victims, passive? What methods were used? What have been the results of such methods?

Regarding these issues, we are witnessing the emergence and adoption of a new political and strategic message based on human rights and citizenship, which the digital revolution, that of ICTs, is reinforcing. The purpose of this study is to clarify the conceptual and methodological bases of that message.

## 10 years of digital revolution

The African information society has been established in francophone Africa for about 10 years.[3] The information 'revolution' is now a reality; although, while the customs and practices of the information age[4] have since become relatively commonplace, their essential consequences, in terms of impacts on the lives of people and communities, have not been identified by everybody, be they politicians, decision-makers, or the populations, youth, 'elders', women and men. How do the new realities of the information society – or, rather, the knowledge society[5] – drastically change, for better and for worse, the development issues? How can they be anticipated or encouraged, in terms of political and strategic planning? How do we formulate and express the visions, concepts and methodologies that these new issues are introducing and imposing? How is the role of the various actors of FGM changing, including those who have been traditionally excluded from the action, such as the so-called unproductive people, including youth, women and those people considered inactive? What changes can be expected from these innovations, in a historical, political, economic, social and cultural context that apparently should be taken into account (Giraud, 2008)?

## Combining different approaches

In Africa, the practice of FGM, in the final analysis, looks like a magnifying mirror, revealing (among other things[6]) structural, cultural and imaginary changes caused by the major qualitative innovation represented by ICTs. Such innovations should be expected, hoped for, guided and supported for the benefit of the majority, particularly young girls and boys who are already potential elders. This hypothesis allows us to reconsider the vision, policy and practice of FGM from gender, generational, citizenship, democratic and governance perspectives with 'ICT-sensitive lenses'. How can we use the new reality of ICTs to make significant progress towards the abandonment of FGM in francophone West Africa? How far, why and how can the youth be relied on? What are the likely consequences for gender relations? What can be learned with respect to the promotion of the practice of citizenship? How are we to guide strategic recommendations on the optimal contribution of ICTs to the promotion of the abandonment of FGM in francophone Africa, relying on the youth and encouraging gender equality?

## Looking for convergence

The research project entitled 'Contribution of ICTs to the Abandonment of FGM in Francophone West Africa: The Citizenship Role of Youth' was implemented by ENDA in 2006-08, with the support of the IDRC, according to a qualitative, collaborative, participatory, transdisciplinary and federative approach. It was conducted experimentally with three youth groups in three communities practising FGM in francophone West Africa that had access to ICTs, in order to find answers to the questions posed. This publication presents the main findings of the research, which was quite thrilling, in terms of the many actors who took part in it and the scope of the vision it culminated in. The research project showed that in the era of the African information society, the abandonment of FGM in Africa will necessarily involve the ownership by the youth of the concept of gender and the globalised citizenship space created by the ICTs, an approach implying a cross-cutting, rather than a fragmented, vision of development.

The report first presents the background to the current issues of FGM, gender and intergenerational relations, citizenship and globalisation, ICTs and the African information society, before discussing the methodology used to conduct the research. It then deals with the problem defined and enriched by the study as a cross-cutting paradigm in which development issues such as FGM, gender, citizenship, youths and ICTs, hitherto treated as separate subjects, are organically interlinked. The next section discusses the consequences of this vision in terms of research approaches. Finally, a summary of the main political and strategic recommendations is proposed.

# FGM:
# Broadening the viewpoint

The issue of FGM has always been considered 'sensitive' (meaning dangerous), which has deeply affected the way it has been approached and addressed. This chapter tries to find out why and to analyse critically the concepts and visions that have prevailed in the area of FGM with a view to proposing new avenues of reflection.

## Viewpoints

The purpose of this study is not to provide a historical, geographical or typological perspective on the practice of FGM,[1] nor a report on the interventions that have been conducted over the past 25 years in a bid to put a stop to it (ENDA, 2007a), but to develop a few visions while highlighting the main viewpoints that have determined perceptions, and therefore actions, on this topic.

- Female circumcision was first perceived as one of the manifestations of tradition, considered from outside as 'barbarian' (by an Ancient Greek traveller, for whom all non-Greeks were barbarians) or 'strange' (by the missionaries of the colonial era), and defended from inside as a cultural or religious – and central – *value*. Such a viewpoint based on distancing (or its opposite, identification) and judgement is bound to lead to antagonism, conflict, with inevitable political consequences. Currently, in line with the results achieved through the tireless efforts of supporters of the health arguments (see below), a major change is under way. The highest authorities of the Muslim world have declared (though they have not yet sufficiently publicised it) that female circumcision is not a religious prescription, while refusing to criminalise it (Al Azhar University, 2006, 2008). Nowadays, FGM is defended only by the supporters of tradition, the self-styled 'resistants'[2] or traditionalists. But what is tradition? Who formulates it and where?

• In the early 1980s, people highlighted the harmful effects of the practice on human health, considered as the 'lowest common denominator' able to play a unifying role among all the parties concerned. This approach resulted from the fact that the main strategies conducted in a coordinated manner were led by medical and health professionals in the broad sense: the various specialists in maternal and child health,[3] human reproduction and demography. This limited view of FGM had the advantage of mobilising coordinated action (field, political, legislative, medical), and particularly the descriptive knowledge of FGM and its consequences (prevalence, distribution, effects, reasons, knowledge, attitudes and practices). On the other hand, it had the disadvantage of putting knowledge of and expertise on FGM *outside* the circles where it is considered to represent a 'problem'. Hence, (1) the rhetoric on FGM was remote, based on *judgement*; (2) a body of experts in institutions focusing on research, evaluation, decision-making, communication, and operating according to sectorial issues and methodologies, became a power and decision-making centre outside of the communities where FGM was practised; (3) as the practice was perceived as a matter of personal choice affecting women and children, the community members sought as partners in the campaign against FGM were those very men and women who had authority over women and children: mothers, elderly women, circumcisers; the male decision-makers, including political leaders at all levels, religious leaders, communicators. Such a situation has two drawbacks: (a) it ignores the fact that, in terms of decision-making, the individual is largely subject to the community, and (b) it marginalises all those who have no power in the community, including women and youth, and in particular young girls. Despite its initial advantages, the health-based approach revealed its limitations in terms of citizenship and, therefore, of sustainable development, as seen in the medicalisation of the practice[4] and the abandonment of the 'drop the knife' strategy targeting circumcisers.[5]

- The stigmatisation of the practice of FGM as a violent, discriminatory and sexist practice and a denial of rights was expressed by feminists and human rights movements in the series of major international and regional conferences held in the 1980s and 1990s, which led to a number of international and regional conventions. The rights-based approach for the protection of women and children was broadly adopted by the institutions working on the issue of FGM, particularly in terms of addressing the legal dimension. However, it reinforced the portrayal of FGM as a victimising practice, with all the pernicious consequences such a perception can produce.[6]

- Similarly, it would seem that the analysis of FGM in gender terms did not extend outside of the framework of feminist analysis. FGM is mainly considered 'women's business' which only concerns men in so far as they have public decision-making power over the status of women, not as a matter concerning the male gender as such, including in private, and not just vicariously. The failure to analyse FGM as a gender issue, concerning both sexes and not only women, may help explain why the practice has still not been entirely abandoned after a quarter of a century of determined public efforts.

7

---

**BOX 1.1** Six key elements of change

The abandonment of female genital cutting/FGM: six key elements for change and for promoting the speedy collective dropping of the practice (UNICEF, 2005b):

1. A non-coercive and non-critical approach whose primary objective is respect for human rights and empowerment of women and girls, particularly in terms of health and education.
2. The collective awareness of the damage caused by the practice.
3. The collective decision to abandon the practice as the choice of a group capable of organising and implementing group projects.
4. The explicit community and public declaration of the collective commitment to abandon female circumcision and FGM.
5. A methodical communication process that triggers a dynamic social movement that can help speed up and promote abandonment of the practice.
6. A public political, civilian and media context conducive to change: appropriate measures and social legislation, sensitisation campaigns and programmes.

---

The approach that has guided the efforts of Tostan[7] over the past 15 years or so reveals a major conceptual difference. Based on a positive, holistic, participatory vision relying on shared human rights values and collective negotiation, with much to offer in respect of citizenship, it has been able to prove its relevance in terms of sustainable development and effectiveness (UNICEF, 2008), to the extent that international institutions draw inspiration from it to recommend new intervention strategies (see Box 1.1), and Senegal decided to adopt it as the national strategy (République du Sénégal, 2008).

## Protagonists, policies and strategies

In the past 25 years, the main actors involved in the public efforts against FGM have been primarily women: those active in promoting the status of African women, and feminists, particularly African feminists.[8] They operated within civil society organisations (NGOs and women's NGOs, assisted by CBOs), which stimulated and partnered with the public authorities in charge of health and women's and children's affairs (ministries, national mechanisms, specific governmental organs[9]). Regional and international bilateral and multilateral[10] cooperation institutions involved in these areas, as well as demography, public development policies,[11] including those of the United Nations system, lent them their support. These activists based their strategies on the findings of the studies conducted by international or regional, private or semi-public reproductive health research institutions. In their interventions, all their activities sought, in addition to sensitising women, to include decision-makers at all levels (including First Ladies and legislators), opinion leaders (religious and community), communicators (including traditional ones). However, it is worth noting that the communities were included as 'targets/beneficiaries' and not as actors in the implementation of the programmes designed and financed by the institutions.

The policies and strategies focused on were:

- Sensitisation, social communication and political and community advocacy: through IEC strategies (chat groups, radio and television programmes, national days, publications, films, conferences, declarations, campaigns), with messages designed by health and social communication experts, aimed at changing individual behaviours by teaching about the dangers of the practice.
- Preventive health education, through sex education (demonstration models, publications, etc.) for women of childbearing

age or older, included in family life education (in Senegal) for public school children, and, in certain countries,[12] the provision of remedial surgery.

- Research (statistical, sociological, clinical) aimed at learning more about the scope of the practice of FGM, the level of knowledge, attitudes and practices of the populations that perform the practice, and evaluation of the impacts of policies, strategies and field interventions.

- Legal action and laws that prohibit FGM and punish, in some countries (Burkina Faso, Senegal), but not all (Mali), those who practise and/or commission it. The impact of this strategy has been very controversial, but is becoming less so, the current trend being the preparation of a regional 'model law' that harmonises the prohibition, criminalisation and punishment of FGM.[13] It is not so much the relevance of the legal prohibition of the practice that should be questioned here, but the manner in which it is decided, from the 'top', with emphasis on the criminal sanction that is difficult to enforce and is easily avoided by 'traditionalists' by crossing the border.

- Community action, making the public collective declaration of abandoning FGM a (possible) consequence of human rights education. This strategy, quite unlike the previous ones, relies on a positive approach aimed at raising full collective awareness about the importance of people in their communities, identifying matchmaking networks, and game theory,[14] whose main advantage, in collective development terms, is that all parties win at the same time.

## Debate between the unspoken and the unspeakable?

In the light of these approaches, the question that comes to mind is: what communication makes it possible to discuss female

## DRAWING BOARD 1.1  The unspeakable and the unspoken

'After circumcision, sadness.'

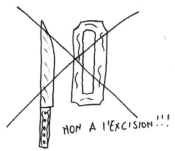

'No to circumcision!!!'

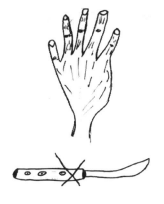

'All my sisters are dead and Granny is unconscious and papa does not know why. What shall I do, otherwise it will be my turn soon. PLEASE HELP ME.'

'I was born with it, and I want to die with it. Why remove it from me?'

circumcision? What is the terminology used? Female circumcision affects the genitalia of women, the sexuality of both sexes, men and women, the private parts of the body and the senses. In that regard, talking about private matters demands special care and may provide the basis for a new abandonment strategy. But is it possible, and how does one talk in public about private matters, concerning the flesh, practices and subjects that are taboo because they are buried under the seal of the unspeakable, out of modesty and respect, which are cultural values central to francophone African communities? Should one resort to round-about ways and other rhetorical devices[15] that divert attention from the crudeness and/or cruelty of the practice – the cutting, from conscious human beings, of the organ of sexual pleasure? Or should one try to draw attention to the purpose that would justify it: purification, beautification, tradition (Sembene, 2005)? Or should one perhaps use technical language that is insensitive, but definitely not neutral,[16] such as medical jargon.[17] To recall the real-life experience of this violence endured by women, should one indulge in the use of strong images (mutilation, cutting[18]), even if it means hiding the apparent intention of the practice (to honour)? The most recent theory, popularised by Tostan, is that female circumcision is intended to guarantee the capacity of girls to marry (and therefore to perpetuate the family name): how can one detect this in the rhetoric and practices of the various individual and collective actors?

On the one hand, there is the unnamed,[19] the 'unspoken', the nameless (see Drawing Board 1.1), which reveals the inability to think outside of a sacred, coded, ritual language. The languages of the ethnic groups that practise female circumcision named it and therefore thought and reasoned it out,[20] but the words used to name it belong to the secret world of the taboo, of the sacred and of modesty, confining it to private circles. Hence the difficulty for women who are culturally and physically affected by female circumcision to talk about it in their own words, because they do not know where and how to talk about it.

On the other hand, there is the alternate and contradictory use of (1) the term 'female genital mutilation', which expresses a (de facto) violent act, a (deliberate) violation of women's physical integrity, and (2) the term 'cutting' (*excision*), which distances the act by resorting to a surgical term, revealing the unspeakable, the inability to think about it. Even so, this limitation of language is accompanied by a relentless determination to say, to name, things that cannot be put into words, things that are impossible to say, to think and feel when one is not culturally, ethnically and physically affected by female genital cutting. This impossibility to think, feel, speak about this act compels one to empathise, driving one to sway between feelings of terror and efforts to distance oneself.

Indeed, female genital cutting does not have a name. All the terms used to talk about it are descriptions that are subject to interpretation and, therefore, controversy. Thus, in order to go beyond the debate 'for or against' FGM, it would appear necessary to broaden the viewpoints, in a resolutely positive and inclusive manner. This is the approach that seems to be gaining ground in francophone West Africa.

## Impacts: mixed results

### How do we measure abandonment?

Much has been achieved within the space of a generation. FGM has changed status from a taboo subject, an unspeakable secret matter, to a public issue that can be openly discussed without the risk of heavy censorship. This has happened thanks to the efforts of people who formed civil society movements, working

**BOX 1.2** Dialogue between custodians of the past and forward-looking youth

**Argument of the traditionalists (spoken by an adult man)**

'Nobody can say that the prophet and sacred scriptures prohibit female circumcision, which is in fact a practice that pre-dates Islam. Female circumcision is the equivalent of male circumcision, an Abrahamic tradition: to reject the circumcision of girls would, in the long run, threaten the practice of circumcising the sexual organ of African boys. We were born in this cultural, symbolic and initiatory tradition and foreigners should not interfere in it. The West is only trying to turn other peoples into puppets, by committing cultural genocide. It was the 'WLM' who created FGM. Europe during the Inquisition performed similar sexual practices on the 'poor women'. African intellectuals, 'poor passengers of the Ark', always allow themselves to be manipulated by the civilising mission of the West, the yoke of the white man borne by native infantrymen. Gynaecological cosmetic surgery is in fact booming, turning femininity into a money-making tool. Why all this hullabaloo? If properly performed, female circumcision does not cause any health or psychological problems. Those who are fighting against circumcision, are they believers? Are they honest? Africa has other more important problems to deal with than this superfluous issue, and African women have other defects that are much more comical than circumcision. What diseases are caused by female circumcision? Personally, I am on the side of the traditionalists, and I am free to honour women; nobody has the right to violate one of the foundations of society.'

**Rebuttal argument by youth (boys and girls)**

'We are not going to engage in a long debate; it is enough to be aware of the consequences, and to consider our own experiences. The rhetoric of the traditionalists is emotionally traumatising but useful; it helps us, and will continue to help us, to brainstorm about the responses adapted to our various environments, so that we can be in a position to argue. We are fighting against FGM because we are personally committed. We understand that the rhetoric of the traditionalists has something to do with the generation gap. We are not fooled by the manipulation and confusion contained in the arguments of the traditionalists. Our convictions about the true nature of divine law and culture are not shaken by religion and tradition as presented to us. And the fact of the matter is that the traditionalists themselves do not hesitate to use modern tools. We respect their freedom of expression, but we have a duty to speak the truth. We believe that African culture can evolve, and we know that FGM is an ancient policy aimed at placing women in a second rank in society. Men do not fully realise what FGM means.'
(ENDA, 2008h)

in close partnership with the public authorities. Qualitatively, a huge amount of work in terms of popularisation and advocacy was done with almost all elements of society. Almost everything is now known about the practice of FGM: its scope, forms, prevalence, consequences, justification, and so on.

Yet, can it be said that the practice has declined quantitatively? Not by much, apparently,[21] considering all the efforts made.

It is difficult, however, and perhaps not even very useful, to answer that question. Since the practice of FGM is perceived as a matter for individual decision – mainly that of mothers regarding the sexuality of their daughters – the monitoring/evaluation methodologies adopted focused on the quantitative aspect of the status or intentions of those who perform or are subjected to the practice. This bias prompted a number of reservations in terms of reliability. Indeed, for ethical reasons, most of the studies relied on what people say rather than on direct observation. And it is not easy to extrapolate the results of studies that are often limited in scope and are conducted with different objectives and methodologies.

The conceptual innovation deriving from the discovery of the fact that FGM is a community practice which goes beyond the capacity of individuals to make decisions radically changes these conventional monitoring/evaluation methodologies. Indeed, the success of this approach is measured by the number of public community declarations calling for the collective abandonment of FGM,[22] rather than by the statistics of the number of people circumcised. This impact evaluation method has also been largely challenged due to doubts about the accuracy of the estimate of the number of villages that practise FGM, and because violations of the decision have been reported in many villages that publicly made declarations against FGM. Resistance to the collective decision usually takes the form of migration to neighbouring communities, countries or regions where FGM is not prohibited, which is now the basis of the main argument for integrating African policies aimed at legally banning FGM. Much work certainly remains to be done, in terms of designing an evaluation methodology for the abandonment of FGM able to take into account all aspects of the issue, bringing together public and private realms, individual, national and local statistics, and other indicators such as the collective determination of the community, criminal prosecution and legal sanction, and so on.

## Reversing the policymaking order

The women's organisations that pioneered the fight against FGM found their strongest allies in regional and international organisations. Won over by their advocacy, the latter adopted international and regional conventions,[23] whose provisions were expected to be domesticated into national legislations and implemented by local courts. The limitations of such a process, imposed from above with very little provision for participation, were soon obvious at the local level when it came to implementing the laws on FGM in the countries that adopted them.[24] Indeed, such processes express political principles that are not very participatory, endorsing the primacy of man-made, positive law and the society that made it over the natural Law and the person, as well as that of duties over rights.[25] This has consequences for the perception of the meaning and significance of citizenship and social cohesion.

The methodology initiated by Tostan breaks with this system by adopting a bottom-up approach. Focusing on the ownership of individual rights in and by the community/communities and community capacity-building, it results in convergent progress in terms of sustainable human development: abandonment of FGM; an end to early and forced marriage; promotion of health, education, the rights and status of women, girls and children; sustainable development; community democracy.

## Modernising communication strategies

The main strategy for promoting the abandonment of FGM, developed in keeping with the recommendations of the international development cooperation institutions since the 1960s for the purpose of promoting social change, focused on communication, and particularly sensitisation, IEC and advocacy. In the area of FGM, as in others, it demonstrated its efficacy in respect of popularising a simple message: FGM is a dangerous practice that should be abandoned.[26] But the arguments in support of these statements were never delivered in public, because they dealt with so-called 'sensitive' (risky) subjects, including sexuality, religion and culture.

Critical analysis of the contribution and limitations of Information, Education, Communication (IEC) (Naji, n.d.) as a development communication strategy underscores the fact that its efficacy remains uncertain, because it is not very interactive, is deliberately unidirectional and vertical (top-down) and invites little creativity. It is often loaded with biases against the practices and target populations of the strategy, perceived as rural populations excluded from the modern world, who have backward beliefs and are not open to change, ignoring the fact that those in charge of implementing the strategy often share those same traditional beliefs.

IEC activities are conducted with the support of public authorities that are not very willing to share decision-making powers with these populations. 'Thus, IEC finds itself at the centre of the power issue in these societies' (Naji, n.d.). In spite of their undeniable achievements, communication strategies, conducted with all the means available (print, oral, radio, television, interpersonal, peer, lobbying), have not really changed over time, despite the recent information and communication revolution. ICTs were seized by institutions (especially international) as communication tools[27] for exchanging information between institutions and experts, but seldom for intervention strategies, with the notable exception of the Stopfgmc website coordinated by AIDOS for the benefit of the media. The main innovation contributed by the digital revolution, that of interactivity and hypertext, has not been identified, nor used as a cultural, political and strategic innovation, which is particularly unfortunate and damaging in terms of community communication and political action. Further, communication strategies have mainly targeted mature women, organised in collectives, and women and men in a situation of 'power'. Youth has only been marginally involved in interventions, never in decision-making. While they have 'got' the message that FGM is risky and harmful, they are not, for all that, fully informed about the dangers and issues involved.

# Clarifying the concepts and issues

The gender issue has most often been seen as concerning mainly, if not exclusively, women. The generation concept is still largely ignored, to the detriment of the youth.

The idea of citizenship, as well as the related ones of democracy and governance, is considered too 'political' (sensitive, risky) to be discussed without exercising due care.

And the option of ICTs as a development issue is characterised by fantasy and imagination. In order to link each of these concepts to a convergent issue, it is necessary to explore their origins and see how they have fared over time.

## Identifying the biases

With the hindsight of 25 years of commitment to the struggle for the abandonment of FGM, it is now easier to identify the cognitive (visions, concepts), cultural (principles, policies), methodological and strategic biases that underpin the public institutional initiatives and interventions conducted on FGM, the results they produce and any prospects of renewal.

### Women's business, gender issue

The issue of FGM has always been seen as concerning women and, therefore, as 'women's business', related mainly, if not solely, to the female gender. Hence field interventions have almost exclusively involved women's organisations, as actors, intermediaries or beneficiaries. Men, at least those identified by their public office (decision-makers, communicators, religious leaders), have only been involved in the FGM issue as (public) 'advocates' of women (defined by their social roles as mothers, girls, aunts, grandmothers), 'victims'[1] of FGM. It was conveniently forgotten that the male gender, men (by virtue of their social roles as fathers, husbands, sons, brothers, uncles, grandfathers), can have a personal and socially constructed, explicit sensitivity, even though it may not be expressed, to the issue of FGM. They receive a gendered education[2] on this issue, such as 'sexuality is a private matter'. They have gender interests – particularly in terms of decision-making power and active responsibility – peculiar to their *membership* of the male gender, which they can invoke in the matter of FGM, quite apart from and beyond the solidarity/protection role they have (or are supposed to have) towards women and the female gender.

## Marginalisation and globalisation

The status of FGM has always been marginal. Overall, it is marginal as a practice, inasmuch as it was originally confined to certain regions and ethnic groups.[3] As a social practice dealing with the private (female genitalia) life of women, it was obscured,[4] made taboo, unspeakable. When it finally became a matter of public concern,[5] it was voluntarily confined to women.

As a field of research, it is attached to reproductive health, and is studied, in terms of prevalence, by including a few additional questions in demographic and health surveys. Apart from the renewed interest created by its theoretically possible contribution to the spread of AIDS, FGM has actually not yet emerged from its marginal status. Although it spread all over the world with international migrations, FGM does not seem to be affected by the current evolution of Africa, particularly its entry into a globalised society. This marginalisation is expressed by the fact that only certain categories of people – the FGM experts, and, in communities where the practice is prevalent, health workers and women's organisations – are more or less aware of the content of the issue, whereas the majority of the population is 'merely' sensitised, by the media in particular, about the spectacular aspects of the issue. The youth, particularly young men, belong to this second category, including in those communities where FGM is practised.

FGM has never led to any partnership, or alliance, with the 'modern' sectors of Africa: it is, for example, difficult for bankers or ICT technicians to understand how FGM affects them.

## Challenging knowledge standards

Knowledge about FGM was mainly constructed within research institutions, financed as part of the political and economic strategy of demography and reproductive health[6] with public and semi-public funds.[7] These institutions formalise the sectorial scientific standards, practices and methods, traditionally highly focused on quantitative aspects, which is clearly reflected in the profiles of the people and methods used in the research process.

The status of researcher, conferred by the institutions and peers, is both codified and vague. Thus, those recognised as researchers are people whose training and skills are more technical in nature (research protocol design and management, processing of research findings), such that they have a weaker background in the conceptual and critical analysis of research findings. The research principles and methodologies inspired by scientific positivism,[8] based on the 'positive sciences' (medicine, statistics, law), focus more on 'how' than on 'why', ignoring any inquiry about meaning[9] (Grawith, 2001).

In francophone Africa, the observation and research methodologies on FGM have also changed very little over time, very often producing (and reproducing) the same type of research data, results and conclusions, mainly centred, without any dynamic controversy, on the prevalence and description of the practice, the impact of the institutional interventions and the need for legislation.

Yet, in the past 25 years the observation and behavioural sciences (human ethology) have significantly evolved in a context that has itself experienced major changes. In francophone Africa in particular, which has not experienced a real industrial age, is it not possible to hypothesise that the advent of the African information society marks the entry into African post-modernity? The mono-disciplinary approach, applied to the Aristotelian logic[10] of FGM, is no longer helpful in understanding this already complex issue, especially in the new African context. The methodologies that, for knowledge-building purposes, separate the disciplines from each other, while maintaining the distinction between research actors and subjects, turn out to be little adapted to contemporary realities, theories and policies. They would be much improved if those who use them were initiated and trained in the practice of conceptual analysis, critical analysis and reflexive inquiry.

## From the legal approach to community commitment

Considering FGM as a violation of (natural) right leads to the adoption of a strategy based on (positive) law.[11] The tendency to legislate on FGM, developed during the 1990s (Inter-Parliamentary Union), is still far from involving all the countries of the sub-region[12] and the regional integration of the laws on FGM in Africa is currently the main coordinated strategy aimed at speeding up the abandonment of the practice (No Peace Without Justice, 2008). It is a sign of the transition to another level, involving the generalisation of the law and its effective enforcement, or a toughening of positions, as shown by the slogan 'Zero tolerance to

FGM'.[13] The legal provisions adopted to that end, for example in Burkina Faso,[14] consist in criminalising the practice and punishing those who commission FGM or practise it (imprisonment and fines), with more severe sanctions against any health workers involved, and sometimes there is also a reporting system (toll-free number).

Experience has shown that the legal strategy is not the ultimate solution, in view of the fact that (1) the populations who practise FGM, the law enforcement officers and legal personnel are not all sensitised and/or convinced about the merits of the law; (2) the modalities, support mechanisms and resources do not always meet the needs; (3) people do not automatically turn to the law, out of fear, distrust or refusal to report the perpetrators, such that in many cases where the law is enforced there is pressure to circumvent it.

In terms of citizenship development, one may wish to take a closer look at the double role of the legal strategy and observe that the public authorities (a) acknowledge their duty to take measures to protect 'victims', which removes FGM from its sole traditional referent and places it within the scope of 'modern' law, and clearly means that FGM, characterised as a crime, must be prohibited, and (b) provide punishment for those who commission or perform the practice, sanctioning the crime and setting a deterrent example, by encouraging people to report perpetrators and their accomplices with whom they usually have social, community and even family ties.

While it is difficult to evaluate the impact of the legal strategy, because it is still being developed, one cannot help noting that it is related to the globalisation process, increasing migration and the judicialisation of society[15] (Collectif Litec, 2007; No Peace Without Justice, 2008). Does it indicate the decline (even failure?) of social self-regulation by traditional institutions such as the

**DRAWING BOARD 2.1**  From gender justice to the judicialisation of social relations

The village FGM court. Under the palaver tree, symbol of the village square where men traditionally discuss the public affairs of the community, the court panel hears the petitions of three villagers. Two men, in front, declare: 'Stop FGM' and 'No to FGM', and a woman, behind, adds 'It is my most absolute right'.

A graphic portrayal of how the discussion of the Law (natural, absolute) has evolved: what used to be a verbal discussion under the palaver tree by the community (of men) now involves a discussion of the statute (law) before the court. The arguments used reflect the gender perceptions: men state the law, women argue for their rights.

family and the school, and an admission of inability (or lack of interest?) to use dialogue and negotiation to address collective issues: should matters that used to be dealt with under the palaver tree be settled by the courts? (See Drawing Board 2.1.)

In this sense, the qualitative contribution of the Tostan strategy, apart from its excellent dialogue, communication and human relations management capacity (listening, analysis, research), is in the fact that it promotes citizenship behaviours (positive, holistic, participatory, inclusive, forward-looking, people-centred, network-based).

## Reviewing the concepts

The two main critical analysis components of FGM interventions in francophone West Africa result partly from their sectorialisation (and consequent marginalisation) and partly from the verticality of the visions, issues and methodologies. These 'blinkers' obscure central and cross-cutting sustainable human development components that are more and more difficult to ignore: gender, transgenerational and citizenship perspectives.

### The two genders

As mentioned above, the issue of FGM has always been considered women's business, and therefore, marginalised. The fact that gender − male or female − as an element central to the understanding of the power relations between the sexes (Dorlin, 2008) was ignored has consequences. Behaving as if (1) only women are concerned in the gender issue, and (2) the male gender is neutral and universal (that is, it has the power and right to say/create/decide 'reality' both for women and men), obscures (a) the social relations of domination/subordination between men and women and (b) the fact that the voice (vision) of the 'male' gender *assumes* the (natural and universal) authority to speak for the female gender (*Dictionnaire critique du féminisme*, 2000).

Lately adopted in francophone West Africa by women working for the promotion of the status of women and those in charge of development, the gender concept (social relations between men and women) is most often used as a synonym for 'women's issues'.

**BOX 2.1**   Girls and boys talking about inequality

'Men try to give the best account of themselves, whereas girls give the minimum. To have gender equality, there are two solutions: (1) that girls give the best account of themselves in order to catch up with the boys; (2) that young men allow themselves to fall back in order to be at the same level as girls. The hierarchy between adults and youth is necessary because adults have more experience of life, they are more mature most of the time; because respect for our elders is the basis of our education. In addition to that, life experience is such that youth have everything to learn from their elders, and the same applies from generation to generation. For knowledge to be transmitted in good conditions, there has to be a hierarchy…

'Girls only give the minimum because of their low level of participation; they can do better. This is true not only for this project; I have noticed it elsewhere also (for example, in my class)… The law is made by a majority of men for the majority of human beings. Women should have come forward as candidates. I am sure that if women had gone out to vote for women, they would have formed the majority in the National Assembly. They do not participate in class because they think that they do not have the right, or they are afraid, or have a complex… They cannot do better than men because it is psychological; in their heads they think they cannot do it. It is not biological. I do not know why they did not stand as candidates. I do not know why they did not come out in their numbers to vote. Yet it is their right. So, in my understanding, all women cannot stand on their own; they need support and it is from the men that they can get this support.' (B.M., 16, boy, ML)

'In Internet chat, boys spend their time boasting and dreaming about the future; the opposite is the case for women. Thus girls get it in their heads that boys are superior to them, so they blame themselves. I believe this is a policy applied by the youth in this project to dominate in an undetectable manner, like Mr Presi, *l'homologue*. And then I think they pretend to be surprised and regret that the women [young girls] do not want to play the role of good citizen in a project that calls for equal participation. Why is it that every time we meet – during a symposium, workshop, evaluation – the girls participate in full, but when we do so online they are weak?' (W.T, 21, girl, BF)

'Every time the girls/women felt dominated, and it was necessary to raise their level to that of the men so that things could change quickly, but we men have agreed to support these women in the fight against FGM because it is a citizenship role. Should we try to dominate these women who are already dominated?' (M.O. 27, boy, BF)

'When we call these boys "President", it is not because we believe it. It is part of our policy. We make them believe in Father Christmas, who is used to deceive children; it is not reality. Before, men did not speak but acted; now it is they who do the talking. We keep our thoughts to ourselves.' (M.K., girl, ML)

'You see your way of talking about women, for example "We are only supporting you." We see you as a martyr, so in the project you do everything to support us, but in real life you do not. Am I mistaken, girls and women?' (W.T, 21, girl, BF)

(ENDA, 2008g)

Hence the existential and functional reality of the male (social) gender is not, operationally, considered by women, and even less by men, in visions, theories or principles, and therefore even less in policies and methodologies. There does not seem to be, in francophone West Africa, any scientific knowledge built, from the male point of view, to clarify the mechanisms of gender social relations, gender identity, gender perspectives, gender education and the construction of a gender-specific sensitivity. The fact that men, women and institutions all pay little attention to the male gender in gender relations analysis obscures the political dimension of the unequal power relations between the genders and perpetuates them.

This situation is a direct challenge to, among others, the scientific community of gender experts, as well as FGM policies and interventions.

In view of the dearth of reference material on this issue in the specific context of francophone West Africa,[16] it may be assumed that the surprising blindness to the male dimension of gender relations is also due to the clear separation of the socialisation processes of the two genders (see Box 2.1).

## Youth and elders: from one world to the other

Just as the female gender is marginalised and obscured (see Box 2.1) by the universality set down as a postulate of the patriarchal system,[17] the youths are, as a social category, marginalised and made invisible in the society, by virtue of the authority of the elders[18] to represent, speak, act and decide for them. Yet, if sustainable human development is considered as the objective, the need to take into account the visions, roles, perspectives, sensitivities, interpretations and specific potentials of the various generations should play a key role.

Youth, as an 'unstable social fact' (Tourné, 2001), difficult to identify on the basis of the sole criterion of age, seems to represent one of the stages of life defined by psychical and biological processes, social norms, rituals, events, laws and roles organised around the entry into adult age (Gaudet, 2007).

In the context of francophone West Africa, (d'Almeida-Topor et al., 1992; Assogba, 2007), youth as an age group still carry the imprint of the duty to show respect for the age group of elders (Ortigues, 1984), especially their fathers. Compliance with the duty to respect their elders and the traditions of ancestors (including female and male circumcision, for example) was meant to guarantee[19] their integration into the community and, in the long run, especially for the young men, the inevitable rise to positions of power and decision-making.

This is not the case for girls, whose status, even when they are older, will always be the dominated.[20] However, the current generation of youth is living in a completely different context from that of previous generations. Relations to the genders, knowledge, age, are challenged due to the integration of Africa, through ICTs, into the global context, without necessarily creating more equality (ENDA, 2005).

## Public–private: what citizenship in Africa?

Citizenship[21] is closely related to democracy: every citizen, man and woman, is keeper of part of political sovereignty, as a subject of natural, social, personal rights and duties, some of which are defined by the law of their city, community and nation. However, the postmodern vision of citizenship (and democracy) is fragmented into multiple, diverse and sometimes contradictory personal, private and public identities that are still largely characterised by the differentiation and establishment of a hierarchy of male over female.[22]

Citizenship is arbitrarily defined as inclusion in a community,[23] and establishes the social codes that are the domain of public and private affairs governed by the rules of male virtue[24] in terms of equal expression, communication, rights, freedoms, protection of individual members of the city or community. The sphere of the domestic, private, intimate, of 'nature' (that is, what is outside of the socialised), considered as complementary and dependent, is excluded from the field of public citizenship. This space is 'reserved' for the female gender.

For men, the citizenship challenge is to participate, by fully exercising their citizenship rights and duties, in the management of the public affairs of the community. For the female gender, the citizenship challenge entails recognising and being recognised as persons with their own existence, *beyond* the social roles reserved for women as mothers, daughters, sisters, wives, grandmothers, and so on. This challenge means that women must reclaim ownership of their rights, including that of expression,[25] and that deceptive neutrality must be exposed through a gender analysis of the concept of citizenship. In reality it establishes a false, androcentric[26] universality tinged with masculine norms and values in politics. This raises the issue of gender diversity: the citizen is not an abstract, disembodied individual detached from his/her concrete determinations that anchor him/her in the personal and private and which he/she may – or may not – be able to transcend in public. This issue is particularly acute in the newly established African information society.

The periods of societal restructuring, even of breaking off, are most often accompanied by a radical questioning of the perception of citizenship... These changes challenge the unicity and indivisibility of a citizenship traditionally based on the idea of a nation-state. Citizenship can no longer be viewed solely in terms of the republican and liberal traditions ..., examined and

> judged against the yardstick of an increasing interdependence, reconstructed from a series of flows (including) ... communication flows ... which go hand in hand with networking activities. (Marquès-Pereira, 2003)

In terms of FGM, the inclusion in citizenship of women and youth can only occur through the recognition of others, private/public dialectics, analysis of the political nature of private matters, of the ownership of the substance and significance of another's body (including sexual violence and FGM). This option imposes the acceptance of the idea that there is a gendered vision of citizenship.

## African information society: obstacles, risks and benefits

### ICTs, a mirror of society

From the mid-1990s, the idea that ICTs were an opportunity for African development was spread by international, bilateral and multilateral and regional development cooperation organisations and the international private telecommunications sector, in conferences, initiatives and projects. They were portrayed as the new panacea for economic, social, citizenship, community, democratic and personal development, mainly in terms of rights to information, expression and communication, encouraging the expression and protection of human rights in a sustainable democratic society (ENDA, 2004).

Women's organisations, feminists and 'gender and ICT' experts examined this vision in gender terms in order to determine how the African information society influences the power relations between men and women, and to assess the magnitude of the gender digital divide. The main conclusion of this research is that (school-going) youth are the group that benefit the most from the digital revolution, but that gender disparities remain of serious concern in the strategic areas of content and control, much more than in terms of capacity to consume (access, accessibility and training) (ENDA, 2005).

In the area of AIDS, several initiatives have tried to use ICTs to promote change in the behavioural and sexual practices of youth; in that of FGM, the few applications produced (web pages, CD-Roms) focus mainly on institutional communication, in formats and languages that could be owned neither by the communities practising FGM in francophone West Africa, nor by the youth. The advantage of ICTs as a strategic community intervention tool, particularly for the youth, is only now being appreciated (No Peace Without Justice, 2008).

## Beyond stereotypes

The obvious marginalisation of the communities that practise FGM in francophone West Africa within the (African and global) information society is due to the real obstacles that have hampered Africa's joining the globalised world: illiteracy; lack of infrastructure, network coverage, equipment; the cost of equipment and connectivity; oral traditions and the existence of a very large number of African languages. A long list of factors, considered as so many 'obstacles', have been mentioned throughout the study to justify the absence of initiatives aimed at using ICTs to intervene within and alongside communities (including youth and women) (ENDA, 2007b, 2007c, 2007d), by nearly all the actors, institutions, decision-makers, communities, adults, youths, women and men.

But the fact of the matter is that such an attitude is not really justified, and indeed does not reflect a strategic vision. Since its advent more than 10 years ago in francophone West Africa, the digital revolution has spread across the subregion. The rate of growth of mobile telephony in Africa is the highest in the world, and universal access policies have been implemented. Mobile phone coverage in African countries is now close to 95 per cent,[27] a fact confirmed by sociological study of the actors, as presented later in the text.

This certainly does not mean that the global, regional and national digital divide has been resolved, but it does invalidate the general and so-called legitimate belief that it is not currently possible, relevant, interesting and strategic to use ICTs on the issue of FGM in communities that engage in the practice, at least with the youth. One might wonder whether the justification for inaction on FGM with and through ICTs is not another example of the perversity of the victimising stereotyping (including by themselves) of the women and girls of the communities that engage in the practice, but also of all the communities practising FGM, as well as all those on the 'wrong' side of the global divide. This uncitizen-like[28] attitude reinforces the unequal power relations between the 'marginalised' and those who are not marginalised, and is used to justify the current trend towards adopting 'all-legal' policies (No Peace Without Justice, 2008).

More basically, the fact that ICTs have never been perceived strategically as something that can be harnessed by the actors involved in promoting the abandonment of FGM – whereas circumcisers do not hesitate to use their mobile phones to make appointments with the parents who wish to have their daughters circumcised[29] – is due to the fact that, generally speaking, the qualitative novelty of ICTs in terms of communication (owing to their capacity to promote horizontal, interactive and, therefore, democratic communication) is constantly obscured in all social spheres. Most of those who took part in the project did not see ICTs as anything more than the name that is currently given to the means of communication, the media. The confusion about the meaning of this technological revolution is such that, during the ICT–FGM project and on several occasions, people have said that 'the tam-tam, the griot, are ICTs'. Since people know more about how to use ICT tools than about the strategic challenge involved, the latter can obviously not be understood.

# A cross-cutting, participatory and reflexive methodology

To consider the recommendations that should be made to offset these conventional and fragmented visions, as well as to help promote the use of ICTs by youth as part of a citizenship approach to the promotion of the abandonment of FGM in francophone West Africa, a comprehensive exploratory study was conducted during a two-year period (October 2006–October 2008) in three communities practising FGM in three countries of the subregion. It introduced some innovations in its methodological approaches.

## The research project

The research project entitled 'Contribution of ICTs to the Abandonment of FGM in Francophone West Africa: The Citizenship Role of Youth', better known as the ICT–FGM project, was conducted by ENDA Tiers-Monde (Dakar, Senegal) with the support of the International Development Research Centre (Ottawa, Canada). Its objective was the strategic use of ICT to speed up the abandonment of FGM by enhancing the participation of young citizens in the mainstreaming of FGM policies in francophone West Africa. It aimed at determining the level of ownership by communities of the fight against FGM and the potential for citizenship utilisation of ICTs by youth as part of the drive to mainstream African legislations against FGM.

The project was conducted over 30 months within a qualitative and unifying framework with youth groups from the communities practising FGM with access to ICTs and where interventions were being carried out against the practice. The project made it possible to popularise and build the multidisciplinary research capacities of about twenty researchers, sensitise and train over 100 youths, and reach close to 800 community and public decision-makers, who were sensitised through about 10 physical and virtual meetings. The potential impact of ICTs in the fight against FGM and the citizenship role of youth has been highlighted in around 100 research documents.[1]

## Targets, beneficiaries, partners, actors

Youth associations

The research was conducted in three countries in francophone Africa: Burkina Faso, Mali and Senegal, considered as representative in terms of prevalence of the practice of and interventions on FGM, as well as in terms of commitment and achievements in ensuring community ownership of ICTs.

Quite logically, the study was conducted in communities where FGM is a widespread practice and where ICTs[2] are accessible, away from the national capital. Three secondary cities were selected: Bobo-Dioulasso in Burkina Faso (about 450,000 inhabitants), Ségou in Mali (about 100,000 inhabitants) and Tambacounda in Senegal (about 80,000 inhabitants).[3]

The project tried in vain to identify in these communities any development associations already active on FGM involving youth and using ICTs. Thus, the actors in Ségou and Bobo-Dioulasso undertook to form ad hoc associations complying with the project criteria; that is, they should be made up of a minimum of 30 members and respect the principle of gender parity. In Ségou, the association Nietàa[4] was established by reviving a latent project composed of young girls and boys working with an ICT expert, himself part of the local, national and regional youth networks and intervening in the most active cybercafé in the town, with the support of a development organisation working on FGM. In Bobo-Dioulasso, the association Musso Dambe[5] was set up by an ICT expert from a football club in his neighbourhood and girls frequenting a centre for girls in the same neighbourhood, with the support of a midwife experienced in IEC on FGM and youth health. In Tambacounda, where there is a regional representation of GEEP, a development NGO active both on FGM and on ICTs in schools, it was decided to bring together three FLE clubs in three secondary schools of the city to meet the set criteria, with the support of teachers involved in FLE activities and an ICT engineer based in Dakar.

The lists of members in the three cases show that almost all these youths were or had been in school, spoke French, already had a mobile phone, and a third or half of them had an email address even before the project started. In the follow-up to the activities, the three associations noted that every year about 20 per cent of their members, most of them having finished secondary school, left the community (generally for the capital), and established strategies to stabilise and enlarge their membership. Thus a partnership was established, in Tambacounda, with the local chapter of the Scouts and Guides of Senegal, and with a local grassroots development NGO in Ségou.

The research team

Apart from the regional coordination team, composed entirely of women (regional coordinator, project assistant, regional ICT and FGM advisers), the research team comprised, in each of the three countries, a female national researcher (three women, including two FGM operational research specialists and an educator specialised in educational research, involved in women's

**BOX 3.1** Coaching: paternalistic or instructive?

'My wards.' (female researcher)

'The blog requires special training that the youth do not have; we will include youth according to how well they have learned the skills needed to manage the blog. The programming is very sensitive; a small error can seriously affect the proper operation of the blog. The training delivered does not allow us to leave the youth to work without supervision. The youth are incapable of managing a blog/using ICTs. We just wanted to protect the tool, by correcting any mistakes beforehand! The blog cannot be managed by the youth. The management has to comply with a number of criteria that have to be defined beforehand. The issue is not mastery or not of the blog design and management techniques, but the reliability and management of the content. All the same, the youth must make their contribution; all they need to do is create their own blogs and build links to the TICETMGF blog.' (trainer)

'We need coaches for the technical training. The youth need coaches to support them technically. We are the ones who should produce the content of our blog.' (youth)

(ENDA, 2008h)

ownership of CTs), each supported by an 'e-specialist' in ICTs and an 'e-specialist' in FGM. In total, the specialists numbered 1 woman and 5 men at the beginning of the project, and up to 11 people (2 women and 9 men) at the time of the symposium.[6]

The names and roles of the 'specialists' changed throughout the programme. Initially recruited to serve as technical assistants to the researchers and to maintain contact between the latter and the communities and youth targeted by the project, they were considered as 'coaches' of the youth during the symposium, before they were recognised by the latter as 'advisers' and 'elders'. The clear numerical predominance of the male 'specialists–coaches–elders' was accentuated by the discretion with which their female counterparts played their role.

In view of the poor research results obtained in the middle of the project, the composition of the research team was changed, as well as the research methodologies (the latter is discussed later). The national researchers and regional advisers were replaced by researchers and trainers specialised in conceptual and critical analysis in the fields of cross-cultural psychology, gender-ICT and communication, and group and project management.

From targets to actors

The youth, both boys and girls, of the communities practising FGM were successively considered as objects, targets, beneficiaries, partners and actors in the research. Initially, the project arbitrarily selected the youth according to the sole criterion of age (15–25); during the execution this criterion was slightly reviewed upward by the youth themselves.

Although right from the beginning the project tried to cater as much for school-going as for illiterate youth, most of the young people who participated were going to or had been to school. A large number were still in high school (grades 10, 11 and 12), at university, employed or looking for employment in a very broad range of areas in the formal and informal sectors.

The girls and boys were also single, married and/or parents. With one exception, all of them claimed to be literate enough in French (the working language of the project) to participate in the virtual and physical activities, although in practice this skill was discussed.

## From wait-and-see to participation

Asking for the tools before making a move

> 'In the beginning of this 9th year of the 21st century, I, ——,
> coach of —— team, wish ... that this year be one during which
> the project partners named during the symposium will accept to
> provide us with what we need to demonstrate our capacity to
> mobilise efforts against FGM in our respective towns and cer-
> tainly in the subregion.Aa-a-a-a-men!' (List, ICT–FGM teams, 3
> January 2009)

From its inception to its implementation, the project was faced
with very high expectations from the specialists/coaches in particular, but also from female researchers and youths, who were
all asking for equipment and connectivity, financial resources
and training. This request for 'incentives' (*sic*) was due to the fact
that all these actors were saying that they did not have access (or
means of access) to ICTs, and that the project 'was expected' to
provide the means that would enable those who were capable but
unable to prove their commitment. The project never granted
this request (Deleuze, 1986), even though it is generally regarded
as an obvious one in most development projects. In research
terms, this request could not be considered for the following
reason: there would have been no point in ascertaining whether
the youth could use ICTs to contribute to the abandonment of
FGM in communities that practise it if, from the outset, it is
acknowledged that in these communities ICTs are not accessible
to youth; and if, in order to know what ICTs can be used for,
one should begin by 'providing' ICTs.

On the contrary, the project decided to work on the assumption that ICTs – not all ICTs, and not everywhere – did exist in
communities, that the youth were already using them, and that
it was on the basis of these realities that one should study how

**BOX 3.2**  Research, policy and strategy ignored in favour of short-term materialistic, technical, financial and administrative solutions

'It would be desirable for our direct partners to be supported (materially, financially, etc.) for better collaboration … At present, the project has not been able to find the strategies necessary to mobilise the young direct partners.' (female researcher)

'There is no incentive policy, yet it is very important.' (expert)

'Why do [some people] not have access to a blog? Is it due to lack of money to pay for connection costs or lack of time to go there? Or is it simply a technical problem? … What do you need to implement this activity? What do you need to train your friends to use the blog, make it lively and update its content? How do you intend to approach the political leaders, donors, NGOs and associations involved in the field of ICTs and FGM in order to sensitise them to support you? … and to provide you with the means to contribute actively in this sensitisation? … Who should help you?' (female researcher)

'The steering committee [will be asked to] supervise, provide reports and accounts and monitor relations with the donors, regional partner and conflicts.' (coach)

'After the symposium we would like decisions to be implemented immediately, namely financial and material assistance to help our wishes come true in the field – that is, our training on ICTs in a well-equipped room with an instructor who will provide an introduction on how to use ICTs and establish community radio.' (youth)

'The objective of this day has been achieved because we were all able to edit a blog (add text, pictures, video or sounds).' (youth)

'First, we need equipped premises. [We will] approach the political leaders, donors, NGOs … [through] good activities, and at the end, deliver the most earnest requests of the youths. [We] are going to request training … we need serious training for the cause. … management capacity is our weakness.' (youth)

'We need a lot of support.' (youth)

'We should be provided with individual and collective means of travel in order to properly conduct our sensitisation campaigns wherever we need to go. We should all be provided with good mobile phones in order to keep in touch with each other, pen drives, digital cameras for recording content and permanent connection kits. You are certainly aware that in addition to all that, you also have the costs to maintain and operate these tools, especially repairs, fuel, units for phone calls. Finally, we would like to be provided with food rations and health care for every youth participating in the project.'

(ENDA, 2008h)

to use them for the specific purpose in question. Indeed, the objective of the project was not – and this is another idea that people found difficult to understand – to roll back FGM, but to find out how ICTs can help do that.

This 'firmness', though unpopular, proved successful in the end, because the project was able to use the ICT tools, applications and services available in these communities in addition to the physical[7] activities.

## Changing methods

The research was organised in seven phases, the results of each guiding the implementation of the next, thanks to a deliberate flexibility which enabled profound and necessary methodological readjustments. The final phase (setting up the research team, methodological workshop, documentary analysis, field research) counted on the help of FGM research experts using current methodologies in reproductive health: designing qualitative questionnaires (individual, group and institutional), focusing on knowledge, attitudes and practices of the research targets, grouped according to sex, age, marital status, FGM status, community and/or institutional role (ENDA, 2007e).

The initial results did not provide any new information compared to the many existing reports on the issue and highlighted the difficulty the researchers had in helping conceptualise (Deleuze and Guattari, 1991) the relation between FGM, ICTs, youth and citizenship.

The report of the documentary analysis, entrusted separately to another researcher (an academic), provided more viewpoints in terms of critical analysis and feminist opinions (ENDA, 2007a). Overall, the initial research phase, conducted in a non-participatory manner, produced stereotyped results compared to the pre-existing sectorial state of knowledge, prohibiting trans-disciplinarity, whereas the analytical approach provided new research opportunities.

These initial findings were reinforced by observations expressed in terms of needs and translated into research methodologies during the community research workshops. It became apparent that, while the aim is to identify the citizenship role of youth in the abandonment of FGM through ICTs, the 'real' question raised by the research is the capacity of young people to act as citizens, hence the critical need to focus on building citizenship, personal and

44

associational capacities of youth (girls and boys), and particularly their capacities to participate and intervene. This research finding has been detailed in the critical analysis reports (1) of the peer review of the field research reports and documentary analysis, and (2) of the public virtual forum (ENDA, 2008a, 2008b). It opened the way to the later decision to allow full youth participation in the research process.

The strategy of live observation of the results of youth participation began by asking the youths of each association to produce the outlines of the plan of action they would like to implement. This exercise led to their involvement in the preparation and holding of the subregional symposium, the event which provided the first opportunity for all the youths of the three countries to meet. It enabled them collectively to produce the content, virtually and on site – boys and girls together and separately (especially ENDA, 2008c) – and an ICT–FGM blog, a youth citizenship portal on FGM, and be trained in the citizenship use of ICTs, project design and monitoring. At the same time, joint research training was conducted with the members of the research team. These activities enhanced the feeling of the youths that they belong to a subregional community and can participate with the other actors of the project research.

The symposium proved that youth have the capacity to participate in the production of research results, as well as demonstrating the fragility of their ownership of the gender and citizenship concepts, which led to the decision to involve them in the research evaluation process. It was with them, physically and virtually, that, on the basis of equal representation (in terms of sex and age), the gender analysis was conducted organically, described, argued, conceptualised and expressed in their own words, a transdisciplinary development paradigm including the six issues covered by the research, which until then were studied in a sectorial manner (see drawing Board 6.1). It was then possible to propose recommendations on how to use ICTs in a citizenship perspective for the purpose of promoting the abandonment of FGM in francophone Africa (ENDA, 2008d).

In the end, the ICT–FGM project implemented its initial guiding principles: to conduct a qualitative, collaborative, participatory, transdisciplinary research that is mindful of differences.

## Gendered methodologies

The research established the cross-cutting nature of gender at the centre of the research paradigm, processes and modalities, by focusing the methodologies used on transdisciplinarity, complementarity, collaboration and participation, rather than on separation, discrimination, disparities and compartmentalisation. It showed that by emphasising equality, gender comes out naturally as a component of citizenship (the collective management of the common good) and constitutes a major social change in the communities that practise FGM in francophone Africa.

### Beyond the reproductive health approach

Through the participatory, transdisciplinary, reflexive methodology[8] adopted and analysed in terms of knowledge building and power in research, the study highlighted, among other things, the strategic advantage of the value-added that results when youths, programme leaders and decision-makers are brought together, in terms of facilitating the penetration of communities by programmes aimed at achieving development objectives.

The value of the research became clear as soon as it revealed the limits of operational research methodologies, such as those used in reproductive health. Based as they are on normative, vertical, rigid, monodisciplinary methods and techniques that are poor in terms of innovative capacity and reluctant to use ICTs as a strategic tool, these conventional approaches suffer from serious conceptual, analytical and critical deficiencies. By automatically establishing demarcations between disciplines (health versus gender or violence or rights) and methodological hierarchies (particularly between the observer and the observed), they reveal an uncitizenlike practice.

To consider that the observed/beneficiary is just as much an observer/researcher as those who are institutionally entrusted with that role blurs the distinction between professionals and apprentices, now replaced by a concerted, creative and innovative synergy. The object becomes an actor and this in itself radically changes the research dynamics by making it possible to challenge the process at any time.[9]

## Gender as a postulate

The research revealed, during critical analysis of the peer review, the profound gender dimension of the FGM issue[10] (see Drawing Board 3.1). This approach was not possible at the start. Almost exclusively centred on reproductive health and highlighting the maternal and child health risks based on existing medical knowledge, most of the projects aimed at promoting the abandonment of FGM have until now been conducted by marginalising the human rights and violence against women approaches. At a time when interest in the legislative strategy is growing fast, this research once again shows the limits, in terms of results, of the individual health approach.

## Gender relations in practice

By creating an international youth network, the research project made it possible to put the 'gender' concept into practice. During both the workshops and internal discussions, the direct beneficiaries

47

**DRAWING BOARD** 3.1 Gender and citizenship

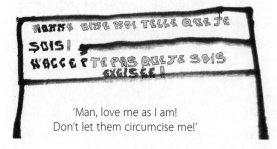

'Man, love me as I am!
Don't let them circumcise me!'

'A good citizen should know his duties and
perform them before asking for his rights.'

'Woman, you have the solution
to all the social problems, so what is
stopping you from doing something
about FGM?'

'We the youth, the hope of the future,
let us rise and defeat FGM.'

created the content dedicated to this issue, were trained and trained others on gender, exchanged views and debated gender with both genders, thus enabling a gender-differentiated analysis of FGM. This approach created a gender awareness in boys and girls and nurtured the strong expression of an ideal gender justice, in both sexes, leading to the voicing of a felt need for action against existing inequalities, even though no common vision emerged on the issue. All the research activities – process, implementation, resources, analysis – contributed, including in their contradictions, to the promotion of gender equality.

## Youth, girls and boys

First passively, as 'information sources', then actively, from the symposium onwards, the girls and boys were routinely involved at the heart of production, creation and implementation of all phases of the research project, arrangements having been made – sometimes with difficulty[11] – to enable the learning and creative ownership of citizenship participation tools to promote the abandonment of FGM. Thus, they were able to claim their autonomy, particularly by designing and maintaining, in a completely independent manner, the citizenship portal on FGM entitled TICetMGF and quite spontaneously and independently organising several chat sessions to discuss, prepare joint reports and brainstorm an idea. They were thus able to discuss FGM in groups, in public, among themselves and in front of the 'elders' of their community and country, which until then would have seemed unthinkable to them, without the information, space or capacity to talk thus in public, or any encouragement to do so. They spoke about the change of mindset that resulted directly in their community, as well as the abandonment of FGM. The project therefore showed that ICTs are a very good means of changing the social situation, in terms of expression and communication, gender and generational relations, behaviours and sensitivities, including in the 'sensitive' (risky) area of FGM.

## Gender parity, necessary but insufficient

From the beginning of the project, and consistently throughout its implementation, the teams of actors were set up with gender parity in mind, in all the working groups and spaces, both physical and virtual. This helped to highlight and analyse the visions specific to each gender. Thus, it was possible to show (1) how each gender has a specific perception of the same reality, and (2) that parity does not guarantee equal and identical participation of girls and boys, in terms of significance, quality and kind: parity is just one condition that is necessary but insufficient to ensure equality in the relations between women and men (see Drawing Board 3.2).

## The silent participation of girls

Collective participation in the project was intensive and enthusiastic, as shown by the agenda of the symposium. Girls and boys participated equally, with some budding personalities – particularly among the younger cohort – making a remarkable contribution and playing a leadership role. However, as soon as the discussions, both virtual and physical, went public, the girls – the large majority of them circumcised, were silent on most of the topics, but particularly about FGM and the actual experience of it.[12] The intensive socialisation of both girls and boys, based on modesty and 'shame'[13] (Morel Cinq-Mars, 2002; Sulami, 2001), explains the difficulties youth – both girls and boys, but particularly girls – have in crossing the bridge between the 'private' and the 'public' (see Box 3.3). It is therefore quite in order to ask whether participation based on parity is the only appropriate method, and whether it may not be more appropriate to look for other modes of expression that make it easier for people to share their experiences and present their arguments. It would therefore be relevant to continue looking for the best adapted modes of expression for African girls when investigating 'private' matters, and to analyse better how far girls/women consider their bodies as belonging to them first, or equally to others or to their community. Girls seem to find it easier to express themselves (but not debate) about such issues in wall posters (Drawing Board 3.2) than verbally.

**DRAWING BOARD** 3.2    From past to present: women expressing themselves

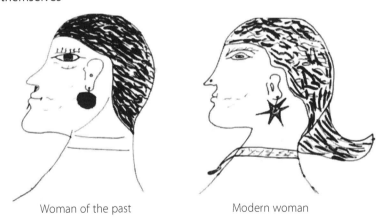

Woman of the past                    Modern woman

In Bobo tradition, to express in public (private) conjugal grievance, a married woman sealed her lips with a piece of wood, which she only removed after accepting the solution proposed by the husband. These drawings reiterate this idea, applying it in comparison to a young modern woman who, despite the fact that her hairstyle and jewellery have changed, remains almost the same, with her mouth closed. Social communication techniques and tools have changed, but how are women supposed to know how, be able and want to use these interactive ICT skills in order to change their status within their community?

---

**BOX 3.3**   FGM and sexuality:
girls talking about private matters in public

'Young girl citizens, your body is yours to enjoy.'

'Youth, be conscious of the damaging
effects of female circumcision.'

'I was born with it, and I want to die with it.'

'Why FGM?'

'Let us respect women's sex organs.'

'Stop! Circumcising a girl is destructive.'

'No Granny! If you do that to me, you will destroy me inside.'

'The youth are listening to each other.
The youth together with the youth, we can do it.'

---

## ICTs: youth on the frontline

### An integration strategy

The technologies that form the bases of the information society facilitate participation, interaction and collaboration in the substantive public debate on principles, policies, issues, strategies and evaluation. These technical innovations were amply taken advantage of by using the Internet tools available in the selected communities that practise FGM: blog, Web, public and private discussion lists, forums, chatting. The youth were able, by using ICTs, to make the transition to a different level of knowledge and relation to time and space. They fully understood that they are in a good position to use them to play, get information, discuss, express themselves, organise themselves collectively and learn. The blog created by the youth for the youths, from reproduced and original content focusing on drama activities and video, shows how much they learned and trained.

## Convergent approaches: youths, gender, citizenship and ICTs

More basically, analysis of the issues (the abandonment of FGM, ICTs as a vehicle of citizenship development, citizenship) was transformed by the combination of two concepts: youth (young girls and boys) as purveyors of change, and gender, which cuts across all social analyses, including in understanding the concept of youth.[14] All the community and institutional actors of the project (decision-makers, communicators, youth) validated the 'natural' citizenship responsibility of youth in terms of takeover and change. The young actors of the project clearly expressed their gender-differentiated awareness of the organic links between the concepts of ICT[15] and citizenship, as applied to FGM. They also gained awareness of their responsibilities in terms of alternatives and long-term good practices in the field in question.

## Learning the practice of citizenship and research

The research enabled the youths to practise citizenship by developing arguments, speaking about very sensitive issues, mobilising other youths to get them to participate, communicating with older people and organising parallel activities. The means used, virtually and physically, led to appropriate training and opened various doors to information. At every opportunity, the youth played a central role: data collection, feedback, brainstorming, analysis, debate, synthesis. They were thus able to create a linkage between the different themes, from FGM to citizenship through ICTs and gender inequalities. This linkage, though still intuitive, has become a strikingly entrenched referent.

**BOX 3.4** FGM research: concepts and methods that need updating

### A lack of gender vision

'These documents [on FGM, ICT] deal with issues sometimes directly related to women, and men only come in later to support the initiatives and help women be better integrated into the decision-making centres, political institutions [national or international], and in society in general.'

### Deficiencies in conceptual, analytical and reflexive skills

'Conceptual analysis is new for us, at least for me.'

'The issue of concepts … is not fully understood by the researchers.'

'The peer review is not understood in general by [us] researchers.'

'Researchers should be trained in this before they go to the field.'

'I must say that this exercise is one of the most difficult I have ever done because this is my first time and things often get muddled in my head.'

'I must say that it is difficult for me to find a theme to work on [in online documentary analysis].'

'In my opinion, this analysis [critical analysis of the peer review] is a constructive analysis, but I get the impression that we failed to get to the point in all the analyses.'

'I am not offended [by the critical analysis of the peer review] because what I said is the truth.'

'I have no doubts about the work that was entrusted to me and which I have done.'

## Rigid normative methods that produce poor research results

'We are executives.'

'I have been an obedient interface.'

'We are consultants, you have to accept that.'

'You have to respect the standards.'

'We have created expectations, hopes.'

'It is our credibility that is at stake.'

## An uncitizen-like practice that establishes boundaries and hierarchies

'We are all prepared to contribute fully if all the arrangements are made.'

'[The virtual forum] was an interactive exercise which enabled the youths to innovate… The forum … showed the innovative capacity of youth. The youth's ownership of ICTs created a genuine group dynamics.'

'How to participate without influencing other people's ideas. Especially the youngest who do not have enough ideas or experience regarding these issues. On the other hand, regarding the laws, citizenship and others, I think we can give our opinion, but in such a way that everybody will understand.'

'It would be a serious mistake to reproduce in the workshops you are organising this type of bias, which our project is mainly expected to address. '

**Reluctance to use ICTs as a strategic tool**

'We are not speaking on the same wavelength.'

'You should think about meeting with us.'

(ENDA, 2008f)

# The necessary
# transdisciplinary approach

This chapter describes the trandisciplinary paradigm brought to light by the research: its principal components, their interrelationship and how to articulate them.

## FGM, a citizenship issue

### From rights to justice

In support of the current prevailing strategy, which confirms the need to 'make the transition from viewing FGM as a social, health or religious issue, to the acknowledgement that FGM is a human rights violation that should be addressed in a rights-based approach' (No Peace Without Justice, 2008), it should be underscored that while FGM is certainly a rights issue, it is not necessarily a legal issue. Thus, the research examined the implications of a strategy based on legal considerations, at the risk of subordinating humanity to human rights, rather than negotiating power relations and opening the way for a genuine gender justice.

FGM is a community practice, performed in the name of tradition, on the external genital organs of women in African Sahelian communities, to preserve the sociocultural order of the sexes while confirming the ability of girls to marry. It is a violent, dangerous and discriminatory practice against women, whose risks affect women, their children, spouses, extended family and community.

## FGM and the male gender

FGM, as we have seen, is not 'women's business': it does not concern only women and girls; it also concerns all men (and not only those with decision-making power); FGM is a 'gender issue' because both genders (male and female) are directly affected by the practice.

Men, in their gender identities – that is, as fathers, brothers, husbands, sons, – are just as directly concerned by FGM, not only out of solidarity with their daughters, sisters, wives and girl-children, because of the risks, suffering, violence and denial of rights endured by the latter, but also directly in terms of sexuality, emotional relations, pleasure and gender socialisation.

## Modernising without acculturating

The main reason why some people claim the freedom to continue circumcising girls (see Box 1.2) is the concern, even fear, that the tradition (cultural and/or religious) of the community, and, therefore, the way power is organised, may be questioned. The abandonment of the practice would mean changing the social order of the sexes (gender marking on the body, through female and male circumcision), in favour of an order imposed from outside (that of globalisation of Western origin). Those who advocate for the abandonment of FGM – that is, the majority of adults and almost all youths, girls and boys – argue that the well-being of people (men and women, young people and elders) should not suffer from the norms dictated by men and women themselves, and that culture and faith[1] will not be affected as a result. Youths, girls and boys, are prepared to step into modernity, and to use the tools afforded by it, in order to change, not cause the disappearance of, African culture(s).

## Eradicating FGM: the gender dialogue

Male and female identities

The gender concept was created in order to refer to social differences (that is, cultural, economic, political, psychological, demographic). (Social) gender is the identity, male or female, constructed by the social environment: it is not a 'natural' fact, but the result of extremely powerful mechanisms of construction and social reproduction, through education and socialisation. Gender identity is expressed in behaviours, practices and roles attributed to people according to their social gender, at a time and within a given culture, and may, therefore, vary in time and space.

In patriarchal societies – as well as in matriarchal societies – men are educated as producers with a dominant status. This status is associated with masculinity and virility, courage, determination, honour, decision-making and action. This domination may involve the expression, by men and boys, of a virilism that tries to prove virility when it feels threatened, particularly by the transformation of gender relations over time as a result of modernity.[2] Women are rather taught to demonstrate concern, submission, subordination, hospitality, weakness and fertility. They are educated to accept their 'dominated'[3] status as normal and to assume the double role of production and reproduction: apart from their economic contribution, they reproduce the species and, therefore, guarantee the renewal of physical resources and social moral values while ensuring the free production of basic social services (care, education, nutrition).

Gender perspectives

The manner in which a question is examined influences the answer to that question. To look to women alone for answers to social questions that affect women by virtue of the sole fact that they are women (see Drawing Board 4.1) – for example, penalties in terms of life expectancy, health, security, training, economic status, political participation and capacities for expression, culture, participation, and so on – means that one will only respond to those questions with partial and inoperative answers, because these penalties are established by a patriarchal system in which women and men play a part, and which institutes unequal gender relations.

The inequalities caused by this hierarchical system are favourable to the male gender, simply because the latter is party to the power relation between the genders. They may also be a disadvantage, in reality, to men – those of the male gender – for example, by confining them to a gender 'role' that could be just as restrictive as that of women (and the female gender). Refraining from considering as *merely* 'women's business' practices and stereotypes such as those that currently prevail in the area of FGM, and analysing them with a view to highlighting the social relations, which are not equal, in terms of power, between men and women, as well as between young boys and young girls, is to have a gender perspective of human and social relations. This leads to a critical analysis of social systems (in this case, the patriarchal system) in so far as they assign more or less reciprocity (of gender justice), and therefore solidarity, between the male and female social genders. Further, it also implies that sensitivity to the relations between generations at the same time is necessary to the gender approach, particularly in the current context of the African information society.

## Gender reflects politics

The biological differences between the sexes establish relations of complementarity but not inequality between men and women. On the other hand, the unequal power relations instituted by

**DRAWING BOARD 4.1** Gender relations, youth relations

After circumcision, I am suffering from intense pain and stomach pains.'

'When I am having my period, I suffer and bleed a lot and sometimes find it difficult to urinate.'

'None of the boys in my village wants me any more. Since I was circumcised five years ago, it has been impossible for me to find a husband.'

'Distress, it is impossible for me to have children in my life.'

the patriarchal system – which establishes them on the basis of subordination (social hierarchical structure) of the female gender to the male gender – serve a social organisation role of a political nature, in the sense that politics characterises participation in the management of the city/community. Hence gender relations are part of the issue of citizenship, democracy and politics, since they crystallise (reflect in a single practice) the relations of power, equality and freedom.

## West African citizenship measured by the yardstick of FGM

### Citizenship, a concept to be scrutinised

Citizenship – the modalities for defining and managing the city, the village[4] – is at the same time a status (a set of rights and duties), an identity (a feeling of belonging to a community) and a practice performed through political representation and participation, which expresses the capacity of the social individual to influence public affairs by expressing a critical opinion about the choices of society and by claiming the right to exercise rights.

This apparently gender-neutral vision of citizenship is actually not so: it is tinged with masculine values, imposes domination, a hierarchy and, therefore, inequalities between individuals, in terms of gender, class and race. The conventions that govern this citizenship are just an expression of the masculinisation of politics, which intentionally separates the private sphere (personal, intimate, domestic), supposedly the domain of women by virtue of their domestic reproductive obligations, from the public sphere, where the affairs of the state are managed, or of the community, where social issues are discussed.

## Will the citizenship use of ICTs win the fight against FGM?

As a gender issue, FGM concerns all the actors in the community and is a matter of citizenship. If FGM was only 'women's business', the issue would be limited to 'equality' between women. On the contrary, it marks them and locks them into their social role of transmission (of the family name), a role confined to the private sphere. This prevents them from fully exercising their rights – not only human but physiological[5] – and their duties.[6] Hence, FGM deserves a prominent place in the age of ICTs, which are opening a new era of citizenship. Youth, girls and boys, together and separately, because they were the first to seize ICTs as a means of expression, are directly concerned, just as much as the elders, men and women, in the private, personal, family and domestic sphere, as well as in the collective, social and public sphere.

## Youth: growing into actors

### Youths on the way to becoming elders

The youth age group follows that of childhood and precedes entry into adulthood. The duration of youth varies according to the length of time spent in school before the beginning of a working life. It is a transition period, a period of imbalance, of physical, emotional, intellectual and psychological change. Education, based on respect for the rules transmitted by elders (parents, adults, educators, coaches, older people) is challenged, sometimes with difficulty, in order to introduce new cultural discoveries (music, leisure, sports) and experiences in an attempt to go beyond the known limits, before joining the world of adults and its responsibilities. The advent of the Internet encourages in youth the culture of communication, meeting with others and virtuality.

---

**BOX 4.1**  Behaving like an adult, when one is a youth

**Youth recounting their experiences when they interviewed adults to assess the situation**

'[It was] fun, I felt like a journalist, an adult. It was difficult for me to approach people because I have never done such journalistic work. When people did not understand gender, I felt I had to be a teacher in front of them and explain the meaning of gender. It was difficult to approach people because I did not know them, I was not acquainted with them and there was the age difference, and people were going to think that I was impolite. I have learnt a lot about the profession of journalism. I hate it when people try to preach at me; what I want is to talk and for people to listen to me. When you go to adults, it is the opposite: you listen and they do the talking. I want to be a good boy, so I am afraid of being impolite. For the relationship to be comfortable, it is necessary to let us speak freely and express all our thoughts without interrupting us. If you interrupt us, you will never know what we have in mind (Listen to us) – Friendship (Let us be friends) – Do not look down on us; respect us. Do not impose anything on us. Do not look down on us. I prefer equality. Do not stifle us with criticism.' (B.M., 16, boy, ML)

'It was wonderful. I felt like an expert on the subject … It is difficult to face an elder; it was inculcated in us from an early age. In the past, only adults had the right and the younger people all the duties, and this automatically affected us, and we are doing it without even realising it. Actually, it is not the fear of being impolite, but the image our elders will have of us.' (M.O. 27, boy, BF)

'[It was] domineering and authoritative: in front of the person interviewed, you ask questions like a teacher and his children;

---

authoritative because you have to be brave to question an old man who is as old as your grandfather; formative because in the end you become a journalist without realising it, speaking a jargon which you do not know how to use correctly; it was respectable. What I found difficult was first the approach, especially with elderly people; I felt panicky. ... Formative because this work helped me understand that I am important in my community as well as in professional life; I have learnt journalism, I have learnt to dominate without wanting to do so, I have learnt to listen attentively. It was difficult to approach the elders; it was our environment. In Africa we were educated in a certain way: that is, the strong dominate the weak; it is 'imperialism'. If we take the initiative and put questions to adults, they think it is lack of respect or worse – that we mean to say that they know nothing. I think that we are winning their hearts [elders].' (W.T., 21, girl, ML)

(ENDA, 2008g)

## Growing up has to be learned

The relations between youth and elders are still ambivalent. The youth would, to a certain extent, like to remain 'good' children who are liked by the members of their community because they respect its rules, which are taught by their elders (see Box 4.1). The elders, for their part, want to continue exercising their roles and privileges as leaders, to control the youth, whom they are not sure they can and should trust – which often leads to paternalistic attitudes – and at the same time to involve them as full-fledged citizens in the management of the community that they will take over.

---

**BOX 4.2**  To be an elder: the dream

'An elder is a person who is a doyen, old man or woman, first born or older person than yourself, someone in a higher category [i.e. an adult]. I have the advantage over [my younger brothers] because I boss them around. I act like the boss, but I do not commit any abuse of power. In gender terms, a boy may be a head, just like a girl also, but at home the boy is always the head. I am working hard at school in order to serve the city. You can be a head in front of your aunts, because during prayers they stand behind you. That is because it is the rule and will always be so. Regarding his daughter there are decisions; it is the man who is the supreme head in the home. Because after the father it is the boy; if he is old enough of course. Otherwise the mother plays the role of the head. A person is considered an elder if and only if he or she is born before me; that is, he or she is older than me and also has more experience than me. Then another person who has learnt a lot in professional life, even if they are inferior to me, they are an elder too. I too am an elder to my brothers, who are in lower classes; it is so in the neighbourhood. My relations with the latter are respectful, executing, dominating.' (B.M., 16, boy, ML)

'The elder has to do with age, experience, even mentality. And you have to politely accept the opinions of the elder or disagree in a very, very moderate way.' (W.T., 26, girl, ML)

(ENDA, 2008g)

---

Further, education in terms of (intellectual) knowledge acquisition, (practical) know-how, (physical and mental) well-being and self-management skills (the capacity to act and react) seems to vary according to gender. From the moment they are weaned, young boys are educated, by role-play and empowerment, to face risks; girls are educated, by imitation, to avoid risks, but especially to manage them. The Internet, despite its pitfalls, should enable youth, particularly boys, to build their own knowledge, without any control from their elders.

## Becoming responsible: victims or citizens?

Growing up, becoming responsible, is to challenge the constraints, inequalities and obligations presented as 'natural', although they are social constructs. To accept them is to behave like a victim, to remain in the subordinate status of children, which has its advantages, both for the victims and for the society that dangerously confines them to this status (victimisation), and for those who perpetuate the inequalities. To decide to act, collectively, to transform the social inequalities into solidarity relations is to reshape the world of adults, of responsibilities and of the community. It also means opting for diversity, including between cultures, genders and generations, and thus proposing another definition of youth, too often perceived as a huge little-known group which embodies the reproduction and future of society, with all the uncertainties and exclusion, as well as the dynamism and creativity involved (Assogba, 2007).

## ICTs : tomorrow is now

### A large family

Information and communications technologies (ICT) form a large family, including all the various tools, equipment, software and infrastructure enabling the production, transport, storage and presentation of all kinds of information, using the recent developments in computing, data communications and multimedia (ENDA, 2004). Since each ICT has its own characteristics,

67

advantages and disadvantages, some are more appropriate than others, depending on what one wants to use them for. Some are more immediately interactive and respond in real time; others are more relevant in a poverty context; and still others are more valuable in terms of sustainability or impact.

## More than means of communication

In the past, the means of communication (drum, newspaper, theatre, television, radio, etc.) were based on techniques, infrastructures and equipment that enable the transmission of information, but were not retroactive (feedback, dialogue, exchange) enough to enable the producer of the initial message and the receiver to interact in real time. While the ICTs, based on the convergent use of computers, data communication and multimedia, are available and accessible, every user at the same time becomes the originator and receiver of the information. This enables everyone to participate actively, independently and equally, in the expression, negotiation, management, implementation, control and evaluation of public affairs. Thus ICTs become strategic tools for citizenship development and democracy.

## The African information society is here

In the information society, the intangible elements of knowledge (learning, content) become immeasurably more important and valuable as tools and techniques (computing, Internet, telecommunications) that enable dissemination and sharing. In francophone West Africa in particular, as in the marginalised regions of the world and in societies based on inequality, the information society is exclusive (the digital divide) in many areas: access and accessibility, capacities, content, control (ENDA, 2005). Yet information and communications technologies, based on the digitalisation of information data, are profoundly changing the daily lives of these people, communities and organisations and are introducing new mental and social perceptions. Changing perceptions would make it possible to innovate and create new solidarities.

## The gender digital divide in youth

The Internet and mobile telephony spread belatedly but quite swiftly in francophone West Africa. However, women overall are one-third less likely than men to benefit from the advantages of the African information society. Among the school-going youth, the gender digital divide is less acute in terms of access and accessibility, but very real in terms of control, content, capacities and gender roles. The African information society seems to reserve for young men the technical activities that are entertaining, and young women are maintained in the status of inexperienced beginners who can perform some tasks (ENDA, 2005).

## ICTs, development and citizenship: opportunities for youth

The African information society should be a source of hope for sustainable human development for all, with an equal opportunity to participate in the governance of all the rights and duties, whether or not provided by law, in their private and collective life, in the community, in increasingly interdependent and interacting local, national and regional spaces. Youth occupy an important place, though they are often marginalised in development policies. It is difficult to give effect to their capacity to participate because of their subordinate status in the social hierarchy. But, while boys know that they will inevitably rise within this hierarchy, girls are penalised because gender social relations (their gender) maintain them in the private sphere that is neither recognised nor even considered as a potential area where citizenship can be exercised.

## FGM in the era of the Internet and of youth

What will happen to FGM if, or rather as soon as, the Internet gets involved? How can one assess this 'opportunity' afforded by ICTs if, on the pretence of informing or sensitising the public at large, stigmatising, spectacular, even pornographic images, videos and comments are disseminated? What should be done by way of planning and innovation to gather people, especially youth, girls and boys, as well as other community actors, so that they can exchange experiences, opinions and proposals, in order to change the situation, by informing, sensitising and conducting advocacy with decision-makers (politicians, in the community, society, family), to ensure that community identity marking is done in ways other than by mutilating the genital organs of women?

## ICTs and tradition: combining wisdoms

Transmitting and enriching the intangible heritage, the memory and collective awareness of the identity of communities, remains the duty of a citizen. But in what conditions can, should and will tradition change and innovate with ICTs? What role are girls and boys going to play in this process, as actors, consumers and producers of content, tools, applications and networks? With what allies within communities, institutions, public authorities?

The new technical conditions (interactivity) created by the new digital technologies impose new methods. Those based on the fragmentation and independence of the various disciplines, roles and knowledge[7] do not seem to be adapted to the knowledge society. There is a need to craft methods adapted to the united global village out of those based on open networks which enhance citizenship participation, inclusion and creativity.

### From hypertext to creativity

The technical characteristic of hypertext, which breaks away from the unidirectional and vertical method of 'traditional' dissemination of information by the conventional media, results in the potential for convergent interactivity between ICTs, as well as between those who use them. This is the main innovation contributed by ICTs. In social and cultural terms, this technical progress redefines the relations between people and their capacities to contribute to the management of communities. In political terms, it makes it possible to challenge the inequalities – between generations, genders, people, communities, nations, cultures – and to revisit the objectives, methods and means of sustainable personal and collective human development. In strategic terms, it provides the opportunity, even highlights the need, to stimulate creativity, particularly in those who have been penalised by marginalisation, to seize the opportunity of a future in which they have a direct and active part.

## How to change?

### Innovating in the knowledge society

Information is the organisation of data into messages, but knowledge involves people, representational systems and values. The knowledge society and knowledge economics are developing with technological progress (including ICTs), exchanges, networks and globalisation. The knowledge society compels innovation: it is less a matter of information flow and the networks that support it, than knowledge, expertise, creativity, innovation and awareness. The status of innovator is indeed less than ever before reserved for those who make it their profession (Kaplan, 2005). However, because the information society is characterised

71

more by economics than by philanthropy, it is, within the tele-communications sector, stimulated more by what is called a 'market' (supply and demand between countries and, especially, private companies). Thus the boundaries between economic and social innovation become blurred, and the same is true between innovation and usage, dealer and non-dealer.

## Innovating in African communities

The recent and energetic penetration by ICTs (mobile phone, Internet) in African communities sheds a new light on the collaborative, concrete and/or virtual practices and strategies, in information, knowledge, exchange, organisation and transformation of knowledge, know-how and interpersonal skills, including networking, between people and states. The community identity is based on tradition, the duty to transmit and enhance the value of content and of the collective memory, whereas the content transmitted by ICTs is often produced outside the communities and is not always to their advantage. The content changes the relations between the male and female genders and the generations of youths and elders. The African communities – and the people who constitute them – would benefit more from the information society by innovating according to their needs in the production of usage and content, than by just consuming the equipments, applications and content proposed from outside.

## New society, new paradigm

By providing the capacity to inform, communicate, exchange, to come together and act faster, further, with greater ease, ICTs represent a new opportunity for the personal development of youth, girls and boys, for collective, community development, for Africa. In the era of globalisation, thinking globally about FGM, gender, citizenship, youths and ICTs is to consider comprehensively the development issue for future African communities, those of the youth of today (see Box 4.3). It also means linking these five concepts and freeing them from the compartments where some would like to leave them so that they can better compartmentalise people[8] and methods.[9] FGM, gender, citizenship, youth and ICTs interact, intersect and interconnect, which allows a cross-cutting vision that breaks with a vertical[10] and uniform[11] vision of the world.

## Placing a high premium on creativity

Transdisciplinary and cross-cutting analyses of six major development issues (FGM, ICTs for development, citizenship, youth, gender, the political integration of Africa) are ushering in a new development paradigm in the digital age. According to this perception, practices such as FGM and ICTs, in the context of globalisation induced by the information society, of which youth, girls and boys are expected to be active stakeholders, reveal the dialectics of diversity and the highlighting of political matters through citizenship practices and, therefore, also relating to gender: the digital age imposes a quantum leap in terms of perception that is necessarily transdisciplinary, and that inevitably relies on creativity. Development is no longer confined to institutional and/or civilian circles, nor the private sector of the economy, all more often than not headed or guided by adults, but now involves more inclusive citizenship circles, even though this trend still needs to be consolidated.

By using ICTs to express their expectations and needs, youth and their elders have redefined their idea of development. Hypnotised by their confinement in the category of development project 'beneficiaries' and maintained in the position of helpless victims in waiting, confronted with the obstacles and constraints (of the digital divide) caused by the African information society,[12] their

**BOX 4.3**   The transdisciplinary paradigm as seen by youth

'The primary element – gender in this case – represents the youth; youth are central because all the other themes are first used by the youth and are also transdisciplinary. All the different themes are in close collaboration. What a coincidence! … Let's assume that a motorbike represents a youth, the fuel represents gender, and the road represents ICTs. The owner of the motorbike is FGM; citizenship is the country where the owner lives. Without the motorbike you cannot work with the other elements; without the fuel the motorbike cannot run; without the road, fuel, owner, it does not make any sense. Without the owner you cannot even talk about the other elements; without a country all the others will kill each other out of wickedness. All this means that all these issues are complementary and indissociable; if you take one of them away, the others will fall.' (W.T., 21, girl, BF)

'The fight against FGM is for the benefit of youth, so it is essential for them to be present. The way FGM is seen is negative. The ICTs are the best means of providing information and sophisticated communication which directly reaches the target and is reliable. Gender: because both sexes are involved in this fight; it is during the fight that gender inequality will disappear, so gender is important. Citizenship: because it is important in associational life; it is transparency; it is respect for the rules.' (B.M., 16, boy, ML)

'All peoples need solid hands. In addition [youth are] the future fathers and mother of families, therefore new leaders. Everything about women has always been taboo. And especially in Africa we are not invited to take part in decision-making. Women just endured. No more suffering for women: enough. The world has changed, science is progressing in leaps and bounds, and why

> gather birds together if you are afraid of the noise of their wings? Information should flow like the rising sun. Gender relations should be better because practice has shown that two together are always better. Why fight with one hand when you have two?' (F.B., 20, girl, SN)
>
> (ENDA, 2008g)

roles have changed because of their participation in the research process. Placing emphasis on capacity-building for change, innovation and adaptation (of actors, issues and processes) has made it possible to avert the potential loss of enthusiasm and creativity of youth, as well as of the general momentum generated by the research.

On the other hand, other real obstacles to the use of ICTs in a citizenship perspective have not been sufficiently recognised or assimilated, such as the instinctive use of ICTs as tools and techniques (websites, blogs, mobile phones) rather than taking advantage of their strategic potentials for citizenship action in order to promote the abandonment of FGM, change or another development model.

Similarly, the container/content dialectic remains to be developed and popularised, in order to make the transition from a consumerist vision of ICTs to their citizenship and political use, and to enable genuine ownership of the information society and its economic, political, social and cultural challenges.

## 5 Innovating: politicising the private and including the masculine

This chapter discusses the main outcomes of the ICT–FGM project. They show that for ICTs to be used by youth, girls and boys, in the communities practising FGM in Africa, and to promote the abandonment of FGM, the main thrust should focus on innovation, understanding the political dimension of the private, and inclusion of the masculine in the analysis of gender relations.

### Innovating as a research requirement

The research was innovative in that it revisited the concepts examined; it did so by formulating a problem that cuts across the issues, in the methodologies, processes and actors that shaped the research. In terms of outcomes, innovation is observable primarily in the strong ownership drive stimulated by the project, in the beginnings of a changeover to action research, and in sustainability through actions (some demonstrated locally and in the subregion, by youth associations and institutions involved in the process[i]), as well as in the proposals, particularly regarding personal, associational and institutional capacity-building, and additional activities.

The constant scrupulous attention to gender parity in all the working groups and spaces, both physical and virtual, helped achieve two main advances: on the one hand, the girls had the opportunity to express themselves on a equal footing with the boys – with the mixed results mentioned above; on the other hand, the gender dimension was better perceived and assimilated as central by all the actors, who earlier were little aware of its reality, relevance or even existence.

The decision to favour inclusion transformed the approach and research methodology – which was conventional (sectorial) at the outset – into an intergenerational and transdisciplinary process, placing the different categories of actors (researchers, coaches, supervisors, youth associations) in similar positions as research leaders, producers of meaning and beneficiaries of the outcomes. The project was therefore useful to the field of research, and the field in turn enriched the research project, which is not often the case.

It is because the project was initially designed as a qualitative research exercise that it was – without detracting from the direction of the initial project – able to adapt and change its methods as the results were gradually gathered; without this freedom, it would not have been possible to go so far in taking ownership and developing the concepts discussed, or in recommending actions. Issues, needs and analyses changed as the project developed, which thus led to much more cogent conclusions than were expected at the outset. The research showed how necessary reflexivity and openness are in gender-based social development, citizenship and information-society issues, in order to break away from sociocultural and disciplinary stereotypes and the constraints entrenched in practices such as the reflective process.

The real tipping point, which enabled the project to achieve its full scope, was the virtual meeting of all the actors during the symposium. But it was thanks to ICTs that the project was able to fulfil its full federative ambition, in geographical (the whole subregion), generational and gender terms around a cause that has become everybody's business, although it was not initially perceived as such by all the actors, including in the research circle.

## Citizenship governance of both public and private affairs

Identifying the political dimension

The research contributed to a thoroughgoing analysis of the concept of citizenship, in concrete terms and in the context of West African communities: the relations between public/state/civil matters, on the one hand, and private/domestic/intimate matters, on the other hand. In addition, the importance of an awareness of rights and duties in the community was examined, leading to the recognition of public and private politics, recalling the conceptualisation of the private and public spheres introduced by gender studies and feminism.

It represents major progress to identify the political dimension – in terms of (social and therefore political) gender relations – in FGM practice,[2] on the one hand, as well as in the area of ICTs, as a potential opportunity to exercise citizenship, on the other hand.

Different citizenships

Boys readily see themselves as citizens. For them, to be a citizen means to have rights and duties and, preferably, to exercise them actively, in the public sphere, according to a fairly stereotyped vision that is not well thought out and is influenced by their childhood and by the moral norms of society. They slide easily from the notion of rights and duties to the concepts of laws and hierarchy, introducing the issue of domination, which they consider necessary without challenging it (see Box 5.1).

Girls define themselves individually, above all, as women, girls and mothers who need customised assistance (private sphere) while making a collective appeal (public sphere) regarding the issues: 'it is my most absolute right' and 'help me'. By expressing a need for assistance, girls present themselves more as victims – and they

## BOX 5.1 Feminine/masculine citizenship

### Feminine citizenship: victimisation

Girls are not very reactive on the issue of citizenship, but accept it as a social norm and do not challenge the need to be a 'good citizen'. Their rhetoric on FGM is based on private and personal suffering. They should be asked what they consider as part of their private life, their personal life, before talking about what they consider as belonging to 'public' life, particularly with respect to their external genital organs.

Citizenship organised into a hierarchy – levelled, compartmentalised, vertical, unequal, socially built according to a masculine model – dismisses women's actions, words and behaviours which can quite properly qualify as part of the exercise of citizenship. Is it possible to have a citizenship model whose codes are not power, domination and the exercise of rights and duties as obligations, opening up new perspectives, debates, freedom and equality and including the visibility of the intimate (private sphere), as the cornerstone of gender relations and, therefore, of democracy?

Girls have interesting things to say, but one may wonder why they want to speak out: who do they want to talk to, about what? They spoke to other women about mobilisation, they tried to make circumcisers feel guilty and to sensitise them, they spoke about their suffering as women, their experiences as circumcised girls and said that they had suffered enough and need help. They spoke to men, expressing their demands, were confrontational, used liberating rap music and kinship relations techniques (Ndiaye, 1992).

Traditionally perceived as victims of FGM, girls/women end up acting like victims. In their own way, women have seized the opportunity provided by the project: outside of the rhetoric on gender inequality, they do not see themselves involved in the action and are waiting to be freed from men and/or the institutions.

### Masculine citizenship: virilism

Boys see themselves as active public citizens who are potentially responsible, even though they lack experience and act on relatively stereotyped bases marked by childhood: the younger brother has to be moulded, just like the elder brother, and by the latter, in order to be a good boy.

The boys' fear of a change in the society that they think is to their disadvantage (Demers, 2003) tends to help perpetuate symbolic, institutionalised and conditioned violence that is repeated (Bourdieu and Passeron, 1970) also by the victims of this violence, the women, in FGM.

'If men no longer dominate, it means that it is women who will start to dominate': there is not and has never been in the project any idea about equality in the minds of the boys, and even less of freedom. The equality between men and women implied by the abandonment of FGM, in the long term, is more frightening to boys than to girls because for the former what is at stake is their power and social role (something they are not prepared for), and for the latter, on the contrary, the issue is freedom. This is the basis of the arguments of those so-called traditionalists (men) who 'resist' the abandonment of FGM. 'If you touch FGM, you affect my manly status [= head] … if we give in about FGM, the next thing that will be affected is our [male] sexual organ, which we will be forbidden to circumcise', and this will cause a 'cultural genocide'.

Are girls seen as the properties of boys and boys as protectors of girls? This interpretation remains to be verified: 'We, the men, who have accepted to support these women in the fight against FGM because it is a citizenship role, are we going to try to dominate these women who are already dominated?'

(ENDA, 2008e)

are in fact always presented as such by the other actors – than as citizen actors, without asking themselves, for the most part, any questions about rights and freedoms within their communities. It is true that the strong socio-cultural pressures they are confronted with are an obstacle to the expression of their real potential and capacity to mobilise.

It is likely that the only citizenship model proposed to females by their male counterparts is not relevant for them. Hence the difficulties they encounter with talking in public, which could be specifically addressed, especially with respect to the gender socialisation process they are subjected to. It must be admitted that the concept of citizenship is heavily loaded with masculine values.

## From real-life experience to consciousness: a big gap

For both girls and boys there is a big gap, in terms of knowledge, recognition, questioning, criticism and arguments, between their real-life experience and daily personal, associational, collective and community activities, on the one hand, and how they consciously, deliberately and actively work them out, on the other hand.

In any case, for all of them, there is a confusion between rights and laws, and they find it difficult to tell who has rights, who decides, who dominates, and why.

Youth (especially men) are convinced about their capacity to make up their minds about the essentials. They are aware of their weaknesses/shortcomings, which they attribute, on the one hand, to the dominated status of the child/non-adult in the traditional community educational system, and, on the other hand, to the need for technical and material support – the need for administrative, political or strategic support being noticeably and routinely left unmentioned. This observation makes it possible to say that they unconsciously endorse/internalise their position as 'dominated' people waiting and asking for material support, rather than seeing themselves as 'thinking', 'influential' 'genuinely eligible' actors. The transition from the status of 'object' to that of 'subject', even though effected during the research, was not understood by the youth as political progress necessary for social change.

Hence, the most meaningful concepts remain the least firmly fixed in their minds: democracy (youths vs 'elders'; education vs power; equality vs domination; freedom/democracy vs duties/laws), citizenship (public vs private sphere), gender (participation and analysis from the viewpoint of gender social relations vs numerical parity/quantitative participation of women).

## Scrutinising the political dimension of citizenship

Actually, the citizenship capacity – not the citizenship status – of youth should be assessed on the basis of their behaviours and activities, rather than their 'nature' as youth. This approach requires determining why they are interested, first of all, in public affairs – through political, public or civil affairs or the private sector of the economy – rather than in private affairs – focusing more on oneself, the individual, what is felt, real-life or personal experience, the intimate – bearing in mind that the process is more a politicised investigation than a self-centred introspection.

Indeed, the research made it possible to ask a number of questions. Is one really a citizen if one performs a citizenship action without knowing what citizenship is? Or, what citizenship are we talking about? How is it commonly understood and constructed? Who allocates the social functions specific to women? In other words: is there, from a gender viewpoint, a critical vision of citizenship, as constructed by patriarchal societies, and therefore largely characterised by masculine values, in terms of power, hierarchy, verticality, domination, inequality?

The answers to these questions will certainly be found in the investigation of the private sphere[3] (the intimate; the place and role of reproduction) that is neither acknowledged nor made visible in the patriarchal society. They also call for the proposal of alternatives more favourable to gender equality, which build a citizenship model whose codes are not power, domination and the exercise of rights and duties as obligations, as expressed in all the meetings, and which lead to perspectives and debates that focus on freedom and equality and, therefore, democracy, and include the visibility of the intimate (private sphere) as the cornerstone of more just gender relations.

Thus, deepening the gender analysis of the exercise of citizenship is an avenue of research opened up by the project on the public and personal issues relating to women, as well as the strategies they use to move constantly from the private to the public sphere in order to assume their socially productive/reproductive functions.

## A gendered approach versus blindness to virilism

A gender *and* intergenerational issue

This research confirmed the initial assumption: the institutional interventions and programmes conducted against FGM for the past 25 years, by considering the practice as an issue concerning only '(mature) women' and 'community decision-makers', marginalised the youth – girls and boys – and totally obscured its 'gender' dimension.

It is because FGM is treated as 'women's business' that it is confined to the intimate, the private, because the private sphere (the home, the intimacy of the couple) is traditionally considered as belonging to women. This makes women even more isolated from the decision-making and public sphere that the patriarchal system strives to keep separate from the private sphere. Feminist studies have, however, shown that, in theory and practice, the private sphere does not escape from public scrutiny and comment, and this separation is more and more difficult to maintain, especially from the legal point of view regarding citizenship.

FGM is in fact treated not only as women's business that is personal and private, but also as 'adult business' applied to youth (girls) from which youth (girls and boys) are traditionally excluded. Conversely, by making FGM 'a gender issue', a public issue (in the sense that the private should be able to find a place in the public) and 'an intergenerational issue', the approach calls on the strength, creativity and energy of youth in promoting initiatives that can ensure that FGM is abandoned.

## Gendered use of ICTs

Young boys more readily play with these new 'toys' that are applications of ICTs and are fully immersed in the entertainment aspect, unlike girls, whose gender education gives them a 'repulsive' image of technology, relegating them to the status of 'novices' and consumers/users, but never 'designers' (ENDA, 2005). For ICTs to be strategically used for citizenship purposes – not only for promoting the abandonment of FGM, but also for promoting gender equality and justice – it would be necessary to reinforce an ICT content-based approach that would enhance the ownership/promotion of change by girls and boys.

Girls are prisoners of a double bind that forces them into silence. On the one hand, their gender socialisation into modesty (shame, respect) forbids them from talking publicly about their personal, intimate experiences (their sex organs and their circumcision). On the other hand, they see themselves as participating – and probably wish to participate, or so they say – publicly as citizens in this matter, but have to do so in a context (including citizenship ICTs) that has not been shaped to take into account their needs and capacities, given that they have been excluded from it. This double bind,[4] a characteristic of pathological communication systems, makes them 'scapevictims' who embody the defects of the communication system of the community and/or citizens, physically or virtually.

Since the double bind is a situation that cannot be directly resolved, the only way to address it is through a change in level or scale. For example, talking about the absurdity of the situation may be one way of transcending it. Creativity, humour, or anything that allows spontaneity, is the recommended method of resolution proposed to people who have to cope with such a situation, because it inevitably creates an enabling space that is used in a manner commensurate with the size of the need. To emerge from this mechanism, it is therefore necessary to identify stable reference points (obvious facts outside the realm of impossibility) and communicate about communication (metacommunication), in order to deconstruct the rhetoric, bearing in mind that deconstruction is neither a method nor a philosophical system, but a practice. Hence, certain forms of expression (drama, drawing, poetry, rap) and certain, more confidential, applications, may be better adapted to their needs (warning service, telephone counselling, single-sex discussion lists, dedicated chatting). The question initially posed by the ICT–FGM project, 'What about tradition in modernity?', finally turns into: 'How should public communication tools be used to deal with what is considered "private"?'

## Gender-differentiated perceptions of gender

The vast majority of the youth, girls and boys, showed that they were determined to get rid of FGM. All of them agree that it is dangerous and painful, but the exchanges reveal that

**DRAWING BOARD 5.1** The gendered perception of citizenship: what women are saying

'I, a circumciser, abandon FGM today.
After circumcision,
a girl loses a lot of blood.'

'Ouch! it hurts.
Do not touch the female
genitals.'

'Circumcised girl, fistula:
FGM excludes girls from society.
Therefore we are saying:
stop female circumcision and FGM.'

girls, as 'victims', are perhaps better able than boys to explain why, whereas boys think that they are more effective as 'actors'. In any case, the confrontation between girls and boys in groups easily turns into antagonism. Instances of mockery, fun, sparring and/or rivalry or fighting are not rare, including the adoption of a jocular,[5] or even discouraging, manner. Boys say that girls remain a mystery, whereas girls think it is difficult to work with boys. The research process showed how difficult it is to implement a genuine gender policy: even the principle of parity established and respected is not enough to guarantee expression, communication, collaboration and complementarity between the genders.

Girls, whether circumcised or not, feel concerned by FGM above all as people who are suffering, as future women and mothers, and portray themselves as victims, but want to escape from a practice that does not seem to them inevitable. This prompts them to withdraw alone, or with other girls, into their 'secret' corner (private sphere), which remains taboo and socially invisible (in the public sphere). The only way they can then make the unavoidable connection between the private sphere – the 'management' of their female genital organ – and the public sphere, which is socially out of bounds to them, is to position themselves as people who need assistance; hence their appeals to all those willing to listen to them. To do that, they use the 'health' argument, while expressing the need to relieve their suffering, as well as the 'cultural' argument, expressing their fear of remaining without a husband, or becoming sterile (see Drawing Boards 4.1 and 5.1). They definitely do not want/cannot (apart from exceptional cases that can be explained by individual factors[6]) talk publicly about the subject: they choose other means of expressing themselves, such as writing, drawing, poetry, drama, groups of close friends, delegating 'others' – non-circumcised, boys, institutions, adults – to address the issue in public. Girls/women continue to play their social role as subordinates, including in their efforts to ensure the abandonment of FGM. Like all women victims of violence, they are made to feel the guilt they have come to accept as their own, and are blamed – particularly by their male companions – for their inability to transcend their status as dependent victims in order to become citizen actors, as if they were irresponsible/incompetent, whereas it is their social gender status that imposes this irresponsibility/incompetence.

Boys, in their socially allocated place within the public sphere, see themselves as citizens/actors concerned by the risks encountered by their sisters, daughters and mothers, whom they indeed call their own, meaning their property, assets, 'natural' inheritance which should be protected. They think they are unfairly more active than girls in the quest for gender equality, without pausing to analyse this observation any further or ponder their role in it. In fact, they see themselves as better, thus introducing a female/male hierarchy in the exercise of citizenship, as in the use of ICTs, legitimating this superiority as necessary for society. They reproduce and claim the reproduction of the system of their 'elders' as a duty, a rule, that may not be challenged.

However, they are not concerned by gender issues merely out of solidarity with women. Indeed boys, and more generally men, find themselves in situations and roles – particularly as 'heads' of household, clan, lineage – with expectations, needs, gender experiences, that are peculiar to them and not always easy to cope with. Even if they remain unconscious or voluntarily inhibited in a bid to hide the evidence of the gender divide in society, these 'real-life experiences' drive the masculine gender into a delusion – of power, of being in control – that it is not ready to deconstruct (Demers, 2003). Even in their efforts to fight FGM, boys/men continue to play their social role.

## Virilism[7] put to the test

At the end of the project evaluation, there was a 'surprising' reversal of opinion in young boys. After having promoted, throughout the research, perfectly conformist[8] ideas about citizenship and equality, they suddenly came out in full force to support the hierarchies (based on age, gender, rights vs duties) and highlight the values of 'merit' and 'domination' as being more important than the principle of equality.

In research terms, this 'turnaround' is easily explained by the change of group dynamics in the mainly masculine groups, given the lack of participation of the girls,[9] which internally caused the boys to compete with each other. This revival of their manly confidence that they were socially right is probably due to their unconscious fear of being carried too far into potential relations of equality. Several boys did indeed raise the issue of domination – during the symposium and later in the methodological and consolidation workshops – expressing it as follows: 'If men no longer dominate, it is obvious that it is women who will dominate.'

In fact, there is not, and there never has been, in the minds of the boys any idea of equality, and even less of freedom. The sociocultural pressures are also very evident in the language of youth, which is not surprising.

Essentially, accomplishing the equality between men and women implied by the abandonment of FGM is a more frightening prospect for boys than for girls – as confirmed by the reactions of a few girls – because for the former what is at stake is their power and 'perpetually dominant' social role (which they do not seem prepared to give up), while for the latter, on the contrary, it is a question of securing freedom from their subordinated status.

The process initiated by the research confirmed this ambivalent reality that is unconscious/invisible but socially entrenched. All processes of change have their ups and downs, their phases of heightened awareness and of regression, or even of individual or collective foreclosure. Hence the need to craft long-term intervention strategies for promoting gender equality that also cater for FGM, ICT, citizenship, including training, sensitisation and popularisation, in order to sustain a dynamic process by constantly providing psychological and/or behavioural reviews, simulating absurd situations (showing the contradiction between official/popular and political rhetoric) and recursively exploring different ideas.

# 6 Conclusions and recommendations

The ICT–FGM project was a visionary and enlightening initiative that brought to light (1) the political challenge involved in promoting the abandonment of FGM, reflecting the social gender relations involved; (2) the know-how of youth and their associations as a means of enriching sustainable human development research at this stage of the global digital society; and (3) the need for methods of building and sustaining personal, associational and institutional capacities. It revealed a holistic vision of the various interconnected issues existing within and raised by the information society. By opting for the cross-cutting and participatory approach enabled by ICTs, the project made it possible to implement and enhance a direct citizenship practice, which itself significantly enriched the research process. This flexible and stimulating approach, relying on the trust placed in the youth, by making them the main actors of citizen-led change, turned out to be largely effective and produced a genuine awareness, a strong desire to be involved, while highlighting the gaps, weaknesses, obstacles and solutions that had to be constantly addressed at a later stage.

The project, by emphasising the need to decompartmentalise in order to adopt new research methods and avoid rigid observation methods, made it possible to deepen the gendered analysis of the exercise of citizenship. It opened a new avenue of research that looks at both the public and private, two social roles combined by women, and sets out the terms of the process by which they

constantly move between the private and public spheres in order
to assume their socially productive/reproductive functions.

The methodologies implemented made it possible to deepen
analysis of the issues and lessons learned. The endogenous production of content by girls and boys, separately, collectively and face
to face, helped them to learn debating, processes, brainstorming,
critical and reflexive analysis, transversality – involving renewal,
re-analysis, putting things into perspective, all essential to developing approaches to human beings, social ideas and constructs – and
initiated a citizenship awareness that needs to be sustained.

This promotion of transversality and transdiciplinarity, at all
levels of intervention (basic, operational and community research,
policies, activities and programmes, fieldwork), made it possible
to decompartmentalise knowledge and concepts, methods and
processes, and create linkages between the issues, actors and
spaces. Thus it opened up new strategic perspectives, rooted in
the local (youth groupings), on the basis of which a vast citizenship community and subregional network could spread to other
areas where FGM is practised and where there is a commitment
to the promotion of its abandonment. It remains, in a context of
globalisation (including of the practice of FGM), a good practice
for use in development research, particularly in the communities
of francophone West Africa.

In this project, research and action were perceived not as a
linear but as a spiral and cross-cutting process. This approach
enables a higher level of awareness in terms of both gender and
citizenship.

Stimulating the creativity of the actors, outside the standardised
processes of institutional knowledge production, helped deepen
perception of the concepts. It remains to be used even more effectively in gender terms. Indeed, even though the project stimulated the re-analysis, from a gender perspective, of citizenship,

of its presuppositions marked by the masculine gender, there is still a need to further analyse the salience of manly values and to question the capacity of ICTs to enable women to express themselves, and, more generally, to enable both women and men to talk about private matters.

In the traditional context of education in Africa, placing youth in a situation of heightened creativity (of content) and innovation (to be enhanced through training) shifted them towards a transitional situation, while maintaining a balance between tradition and modernity. The youth found that they were themselves the subject, convinced that they have the capacity to speak and act, but concerned about remaining 'good polite children', in front of their elders, who are distrustful but prepared to support, involve and guide them. This simulation exercise helped reveal both the individual and institutional paternalistic attitudes of these elders, while also bringing to light their tendency to lack confidence in the youth and their need to control them. The decision to impose parity at all levels helped underscore the necessary transversality of gender, which should be further developed through appropriate training. Furthermore, the participatory and collaborative two-person team (girl/boy) approach, by breaking the generational, gender and social hierarchy and enabling the youth to find out how to express themselves, made it possible for them to discuss the issues and take ownership of the process.

Finally, talking in real-life terms about the concepts discussed in the research (gender, citizenship, ICTs, youth, FGM), with new methods (free expression, games, debates, active participation, self-teaching, self-evaluation, training of trainers) and in ways youth can easily adapt to (drama, multimedia, interactivity, role-play), turned out to be particularly relevant to both genders (see Box 6.1). Indeed, the research showed the relevance of ICTs to development in general and to the FGM issue, particularly in

---

**BOX 6.1**   The project as a factor of change

'The project was a godsend for me, to have this experience in qualitative research (often mentioned in theory in my area of work).' (O.T., 30, coach, boy, BF)

'Frankly, only those in my community can tell you about how I have changed, thanks to this ICT–FGM project. Since I became involved in this project my life has been innovative; it is as if there was someone inside me working in my place. Even in class my teachers ask me whether I am engaged in politics, what I have done to understand French, and how I have managed to be in the public sphere? I can say that I have become prestigious without wanting to be so. I owe all that to you.' (W.T., 21, girl, BF)

(ENDA, 2008g)

---

relation to the need to shift the position of youth and place them at the centre of the debate.

It now remains to convince researchers, authorities and decision-makers about the importance of their political support and to build solid partnerships with them. Indeed, the research has shown that the strategic issues regarding the use of ICTs in the cause of gender equality and citizenship action are unclear both to interventionist and research agencies and to the beneficiaries of the interventions, the youth, along with their coaches and the communities. This observation is of course not new. Hence the urgent need to train staff and beneficiaries in transdisciplinary, conceptual, reflexive and critical research, and to invest in participatory and collaborative methodologies. This, however, requires a specific budget line. These institutional investments (in energy, politics, training, vision, financing) should, in particular, find out the principles and terms on which women will participate, how to support them in ways adapted to their needs, and the capacity of institutions to meet those needs.

## Politicising the concept of citizenship in francophone West Africa

The issue here is to clarify how citizenship, as prescribed and perceived in strongly male-dominated francophone West African societies, is fundamentally characterised by unequal relations between generations and, even more markedly, between the genders; and to find out what new modes of governance should be implemented, particularly through ICTs, to ensure genuine creativity for social change.

### Recognising a new development paradigm

Francophone West Africa is now well established in the digital age, in both urban and rural areas. The consequences of this are recognised and studied in e-economics, distance learning, and so on. But it is astounding to realise how major aspects of social life – particularly relating to women, the home, the private (of which FGM is a prime example) – are considered, wrongly, as having nothing to do with ICTs and the type of society they have shaped, the so-called information society. In fact, ICTs represent a major sustainable, citizenship/human development issue, particularly in the current historical period where the global socioeconomic context is characterised by liberalism. It is, therefore, urgent in this context to clarify the issues related to private life, how they affect women and human relations, which are currently not being highlighted.

**DRAWING BOARD 6.1**   The transdisciplinary paradigm of the knowledge society

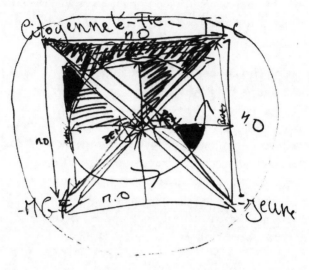

In the postmodern knowledge society of which African communities are already a part, all disciplines are interrelated; they cannot be thought of separately; and action must be based on global thinking. The fragmentation of reality, which forms the basis of conventional (positive) methods of intervention, which partition the social into separate disciplines, does not make it possible to see – or to act effectively – in a cross-cutting way.

Further, since ICTs include a large family of tools, networks, software, services, activities, which are marked by their integration and convergence characteristics, and are strategic in the human, social, economic and political fields, it is important to describe their impact – not in terms of how they are used, but in terms of change, in the forward-looking and innovative ways portrayed by youth in their diagram presented here as Drawing

Board 6.1. It is therefore less a matter of looking for 'what ICTs can be used for' than 'what innovations ICTs contribute, what they change and politicise'. To persist in considering ICTs as 'merely' means of communication is to miss their real import and to be condemned to repeating/consolidating outdated visions, processes and strategies that have not stood the test of time in terms of either effectiveness or social change, and that stand in the way of the transformative potential represented by the citizenship information society publicised heralded by ICTs.

## Defining intergenerational gender policies

In this perspective, ICTs help us revisit fundamental development issues: those concerning individuals, groups and citizenship. When one joins the information society, one can no longer afford to ignore gender, its practice (in terms of both rights and duties), and the place youth occupy in it. It is surprising to note how little is actually produced in terms of knowledge content and by youth as central actors of the information society – beyond the roles of 'cleaning operatives'[1] and 'good consumers' encountered in the project. There is no educational project, commensurate with expectations – that is, at least subregional in scope – aimed at enabling youths to be actors who are conscious of an active citizenship, for example in the area of FGM. The interrelation between gender perspectives and the roles of youth, as mutually interdependent factors of change, is embryonic, which leaves much room for research, interventions and ownership that needs to be urgently explored.

## Collective and individual development strategies

Revisiting intervention issues and strategies, on the basis of ICTs as a factor in sustainable human development in francophone Africa, is also a winning option, because ICTs provide so many real opportunities: to play, be informed, debate, come together with others and learn. Further, this multiplicity provides the advantage of combining collective and personal development. It is in the interest of research and intervention organisations to involve youth as a key resource in their processes, because they are in the forefront of innovation with ICTs, having been born into the information society.

## Making gender parity a precondition

To that end, it is essential to systematically make gender parity a precondition, both in institutions and as part of the routine activities of the actors. It is only then that (1) the female gender can participate, and (2) it will be possible to highlight the undeniable fact that there are are two human genders, with the masculine gender, albeit in good faith, taking it upon itself to speak 'for women' without even realising that it is speaking 'as a man' 'for women', which is in principle a major counterproductive bias in citizenship terms.

## The significance of virilism

At the same time, it is essential to conduct in francophone West Africa fundamental but endogenous and structurally participatory research on the strange gender blindness of men/boys and its consequences for the transmission of patriarchal values.

## Gendered perceptions of citizenship governance

The research found that what prevents equitable gender relations is the fact that girls do not speak in public, and rarely discuss social matters, especially when it comes to those perceived as 'women's business', whereas boys are only too eager to take control and speak out to defend 'their' women (sisters and daughters), without realising that in so doing, while they are serving the purpose of the patriarchal order, they are doing a disservice to themselves as the masculine gender. It is therefore essential to search, test and apply – including with ICTs – new mixed and unmixed channels of communication, which will make it possible to 'free' gender-specific rhetoric and, especially, grant the genders equal legitimacy.

## Building public spaces where girls/women and boys/men discuss private matters

The polysemy of the intimate – what is related to the psyche, the essence, the personal, the profound, the original, the secret, the home, modesty, the emotional, sexuality, existence, being – readily explains the reluctance to see it discussed in public. This is a vast field of research, experimentation, awareness-raising, popularisation, intervention and development that has been too long neglected by development policies and strategies, deepening the divide between the private and public spheres.

## Budgeting and investing accordingly

Each of the four categories of actors involved in the research is concerned. Obviously, the cooperating research institutions have a lot to gain by directing their support strategies towards more participatory, transdisciplinary and innovative collaboration to ensure that gender inequalities are brought to light. They should be concerned about the marginalisation of young adults as development actors, in addition to the perpetuation of gender stereotypes. Consequently, they should budget and invest accordingly, with a gender-sensitive vision, in terms of financing, human resources and training policies.

On the same issues, action/research/training institutions could be involved – budgeting and investing accordingly – in participatory research projects, and learn the new observation and investigation methodologies, as well as how to describe the new development paradigm resultant upon the growing 'virtualisation'[2] of political, human, citizenship and gender relations. Community and local actors, youth and their elders, should empower themselves by abandoning their wait-and-see attitude and be bold enough to tackle practical issues in order to transform obstacles into assets, and therefore create projects, budgets and investments – in terms of training, action and networking – with the support of their local and subregional partners in the field.

There is a risk that one or other of the partners may, in the new development paradigm described here, be interested only in what is of direct relevance to their own objectives. That is why it is important to emphasise that any attempt to focus exclusively on intersecting areas (for example, between FGM and youth, with 'a bit' of citizenship thrown in – areas illustrated in Drawing Board 6.1), instead of adopting a holistic and endogenous approach, is doomed to failure.

## Making the invisible visible in gender, intergenerational and transnational relations

### Producing knowledge content

The research showed how far knowledge on FGM is standardised, rarely updated, unadapted in terms of both content and format, to the needs of those who need it most: the youth. It is important – and this is fertile ground for research, action and training – that, by using specific methodologies (participatory and/or mixed), youth (girls and boys, together and separately) talk about their experiences: that is, produce knowledge content capable of supporting their strong desire to abandon FGM. This implies that the content produced on FGM should be able to reveal and account for the gender inequalities on which it is based, interpreted in the current context of ICTs, as well as on the new scale they introduce, which extends beyond the community to similar sociocultural contexts, particularly subregional.

## Youth at the centre of all projects

The research showed the extent to which youth were enthusiastic, productive, sensible, clear-headed, eager to learn and determined to do something for the benefit of their communities. To leave them deliberately and 'traditionally' out of the debates in societies is tantamount to ignoring an undeniable intellectual asset and to compartmentalise generational, social and political spaces. It is therefore urgent and imperative to involve the youth, girls and boys, at the centre of all endeavour.

## Involving youth, programme leaders, decision-makers and the public sphere

Thus, influential figures – individuals and institutions – should have more confidence in the capacities of youth to act, in order to involve them, together with programme leaders and public decision-makers, in the design, formulation, research, planning, implementation, monitoring and evaluation of policies and strategies. The idea here is to transform the control role granted to the authority into that of a guide, and to draw from the thoughts of a sector of the population which, quite logically, cannot – or does not want to – repeat the patterns of their elders, under pain of giving up its own identity and, consequently, the exercise of its citizenship rights.

## Relations between ICT container and content

While the aim is to strive for the abandonment of FGM, would it not be important to conduct research – especially action/research/

training – in order to achieve a deeper theoretical understanding of the relations between ICT containers and content? And, in particular, it would be valuable to gain a greater insight into the political use of ICTs, which involves the production and publication of content, rather than indiscriminate mass consumption by the information society. Indeed, it must be admitted that the confusion between the containers (applications) and content (bringing to light the efforts for change), entertained by all the actors, obscures, makes invisible, the efforts, experiences, testimonies, analyses relating to development and change.

## Popularising the FGM issue as reflecting gender policies

Furthermore, the research showed that the containers are not gender-neutral, especially when it comes to using ICTs. It is essential today for ICT use by the youth of both genders, in francophone West African, to reveal the subregional characteristics of gender political relations existing in communities and institutions. Such an approach would indeed be a real innovation.

## Social mechanisms of gender stereotype transmission

More broadly, it would be relevant to conduct research and interventions on the social mechanisms of gender stereotype transmission in African communities, including through ICTs.

## Gender diversity and the transmission of gender values

Beyond a mere inventory, the idea would be to make visible the gender (both masculine and feminine) realities and diversities and the systems that transmit gender inequalities, particularly through the analysis of victimisation and virilism, and the relations between these two models.

## Building capacities in the relations between youth, gender and citizenship in the information society

The research process demonstrated that the issues of youth, gender and citizenship are inseparable, in and because of the information society. Yet the theoretical and practical understanding of this fact is not easily achieved by most actors (youth and elders, public institutions and the private sphere). In which case, is it not essential and urgent to conduct research, interventions and training to make visible and communicate, act and train, the actors in what is obscured on a daily basis? Similarly, is it not time to analyse the developments of the information society from the angle of the paradigm described above, rather than from that of passive, indiscriminate consumption?

## Budgeting and investing accordingly

Every actor is concerned by this challenge: (i) research and co-operating institutions, because their mandate involves the promotion of gender equality and concern for a balanced future for the generations to come; (ii) action/research/training organisations, because they should, after 50 years of development interventions, revisit their approaches in line with the changes in the regional and globalised context; (iii) local actors, youth and elders, and the organisations and partners that support them, if they wish, in the end, to benefit from the integration of their communities and if they want to preserve them in a global society where everything is speeded up by ICTs. This implies that each of the categories should budget and invest accordingly in the research, training and intervention processes in order to transform consumerism – which people accept, often unconsciously – into a force that can propose and produce citizenship change.

## Building capacities in gender and citizenship

### Learning and training by doing

The central issues dealt with by the research – gender and citizenship – are those that are most difficult to take ownership of. Is it not time to be trained, to learn by doing, rather than insisting on theory, in order to finally reach the heart of development?

### Forging public partnerships

This would involve forming public and civil partnerships with educational, community, decision-making institutions, including in the area of budgeting. More practically, the idea would be to engage and undertake specific actions targeting ministries of education and finance, so that they can earmark internal resources for sensitisation on gender and citizenship. These issues are the pillars of the policies that it is their duty to implement, in view of their government commitments regarding use of international development aid, human rights and gender equality at the global level (such as the Convention on the Elimination of All Forms of Discrimination Against Women and the Maputo Protocol).

### Building on the creative capacities of individuals, associations and institutions

These partnerships would therefore have the double impact of 'obliging' public authorities to honour their commitments, while building the creative capacities of individuals, associations, communities and institutions so that they can cope with the new challenges of globalisation, the liberalisation of the economy, its crisis – financial and other – and the inequalities it generates (shortage of resources, pauperisation, destruction of the environment). It is a vast area for experimentation, completely new for the subregion, which would make it possible to achieve a quantum leap.

Discovering gendered perceptions of citizenship governance

This immense field of endeavour, research and training, centred on the acknowledgement, inclusion and development of gendered perspectives on societies, would help introduce a promising vision of citizenship governance that goes much further than the simple approaches of e-government or e-administration to which the new modes of governance are most often reduced.

Building the gender capacities of staff
and volunteers of all development actors

This comprehensive approach involves building the gender analysis capacities of all development actors, including especially the training of trainers.

Budgeting and investing accordingly

This, once again, requires budgeting and investing accordingly, on the part of each category of actors targeted by the research: research cooperation institutions, in order to build and upgrade the research capacities and methodologies of francophone West African researchers; action/research/training institutions, to upgrade the visions, capacities and methods of their staff, from the design stage to implementation; local actors, youth and elders, their partners and networks, and the organisations that support them, so that they can be in a position to genuinely intervene as joint actors of their own development.

## Reflexivity and politics: ideas worth exploring

What lessons does the action/research/training process developed during the ICT–FGM project have for social actors, particularly those whose self-assigned mandate is to help bring about changes for the 'betterment'[3] of societies – theirs and those of other people?

Among the main issues raised by the project, which were and can still be considered as innovations in terms of social intervention, one might mention:

- the evidence of subjectivity and the need to take into account reflexivity;
- the gender postulate and the intergenerational as a basis for scrutinising social policies;
- the conceptual criticism of (public) politics, in the analysis of its linkages that both excludes and includes the private;
- the bringing to light of the notion of person (not individual) in the social issue, a notion that could help dialectically transcend the gender concept and the public/private opposition.

These are so many ideas worth exploring, not only in the area of FGM but in all the current analyses and interventions on social issues.

It is no longer possible, in Africa and elsewhere, to continue thinking about female circumcision as it has been thought of for the past 25 years. But how should it be revisited? The African information society is booming: information and communications technologies are no longer a novelty; they have drastically changed daily life and many of its beliefs and practices, especially among the youth. In the age of the Internet, the abandonment of female genital mutilation in Africa is primarily a matter of youth, gender and citizenship: it imposes a cross-cutting vision of development.

That is the message of this book.

# Notes

INTRODUCTION

1. In this publication, the terms 'excision' ('female circumcision') and 'female genital mutilation' are used interchangeably. An analysis of the arguments in the terminological debate is given later.
2. The project chose to consider 1984, the year of the setting up of the Inter-African Committee on Harmful Traditional Practices Affecting the Health of Women and Children, as the beginning of the coordinated political and strategic campaign against FGM in Africa and in the world.
3. Going back to the advent of the World Wide Web in francophone West Africa (c. 1997) (Eveno et al., 2008).
4. The concept of information society (or age) refers to a society in which information dissemination and use is widespread, and which relies on low-cost information and communications technologies (ICT).
5. In the knowledge society, there is a heavy flow of information and knowledge, but the focus is less on information flows and the networks that support them than on knowledge, expertise, creativity, innovation and awareness. The vision is therefore more human, even though this knowledge society is driven by technical development. (http://fr.wikipedia.org/wiki/Société_de_la_connaissance)
6. For example, the written form (texting language).

CHAPTER 1

1. A Web search of the key words 'FGM+history' produces a large list of documents on this topic.
2. See Box 1.2.
3. 1984 saw the establishment of the Inter-African Committee on Harmful Traditional Practices Affecting the Health of Women and Children.
4. Observed, for example, in Mali and Guinea.
5. Particularly in Senegal.
6. 'One of the dangers of regarding the victim as sacred is that it prevents the person concerned from escaping from this psychological state of a victim' (http://fr.wikipedia.org/wiki/Victimisation).

7. *Tostan* means 'breakthrough' in Wolof.

8. The public alarm raised by the international feminist movement (Thiam, 1978) was rapidly taken up by African feminists (AFARD/AAWORD, 1983) in their own identity and cultural struggle.

9. For example, Permanent Secretariat of the Committee on the Fight against FGM (Burkina Faso).

10. For example, GTZ (Germany), Save the Children – Radda Barnen (Sweden), AIDOS (Italy).

11. For example, Intact Network.

12. For example, in Burkina Faso.

13. Similar to the model laws that were adopted on reproductive health and prevention of AIDS.

14. 'Game theory is a mathematical approach to issues of strategy found, for example, in operational research and economics. It studies situations where the choices of two or more protagonists have the same consequences for either of them.... It is used in the theory of negotiation; it makes it possible to analyse mathematically issues which have until now remained philosophical, such as morality' (http://fr.wikipedia. org/wiki/Théorie_des_jeux).

15. www.espacefrancais.com/style.html; http://fr.wikipedia.org/wiki/ Rhétorique.

16. 'Insensitive', smooth rhetoric is never neutral; it gives a voice to a dominant system, in this case based on masculine power (Dorlin, 2008).

17. UNICEF/WHO definition: 'Female circumcision is the most frequent form of Female Genital Mutilation (FGM) or female genital cutting, which comprises all surgical procedures involving partial or total removal of the external genitalia or other injuries to the female genital organs for cultural or non-therapeutic reasons.'

18. There is no exact equivalent in English of the French term *excision*.

19. 'What, inside us, refuses to be named is something absent that wants to be heard' (http://himmelweg.blog.lemonde. fr/2006/09/26/2006_09_linnomable/).

20. Sapir–Whorf Hypothesis: 'The fact of the matter is that the "real world" is to a large extent unconsciously built up on the language habits of the group' (http://fr.wikipedia.org/wiki/Hypothèse_Sapir- Whorf. It is in our language that we 'cast the way we reason').

21. Opinions vary about how much the practice of FGM has declined in the past twenty years. UNICEF (2005a) estimates that FGM has definitely been abandoned by the young generation in almost all countries. On the other hand, Population Reference Bureau (2001) estimates the rate of abandonment at a small percentage only. The two sources agree that FGM has declined mostly in urban areas, where education and

income levels are higher. Nevertheless, the abandonment of FGM is significant in villages that have made Public Declarations of Abandonment (UNICEF, 2008). How can one reconcile these conclusions with those that announce, often without evidence, the doubling in fifteen years of the total number of women circumcised or who run the risk of being circumcised in the world? As summed up by the Population Council: 'Despite its cultural entrenchment, *and even without any targeted intervention*, there is a gradual abandonment in many countries' (Shaaban and Harbison, 2005; stress added).

22. 'To date (3 February 2009), 3,548 villages have collectively abandoned FGM in Senegal, 298 in Guinea' (Tostan, in ENDA, 2007–2008).

23. For example, the additional Protocol to the African Charter on Human and Peoples' Rights on the Rights of Women in Africa.

24. See, for example, http://criged.org/index.php?view=article&catid=29: genre-jeunesse-sexualite&id=52:tolerance-zero&tmpl=component&print=1&page=et (ENDA, 2007b, 2007c, 2007d).

25. On the debate on law and Law, see: http://fr.wikipedia.org/wiki/Droit#La_loi_et_le_droit; www.stephane.info/show.php%3Fcode%3Dweblog&direct %3D641&lg%3Dfr.

26. Or at least one that it is more advisable to practise in secret.

27. Particularly several CD-Roms.

CHAPTER 2

1. 'FGM is a tragedy experienced by the girl alone' (ENDA, 2007b).

2. Gendered: constructed according to a gender perspective (Dorlin, 2008).

3. Occupying the area under the influence of the old Mandinka empire in West Africa (Camara, 1992: 20).

4. Indeed rendered invisible.

5. As with other gender issues considered as women's business: domestic and conjugal violence, unwanted marriage and pregnancy, contraception, abortion, prostitution.

6. Itself only one aspect of sexual health, which does not account for the whole issue of sexuality.

7. Mostly from North America.

8. http://fr.wikipedia.org/wiki/Positivisme.

9. In the triple sense of orientation, sensitivity and significance.

10. For example, 'for or against' FGM, concern about the 'right answer' to the questionnaires, reality as being external to the observer.

11. On the Law versus law debate, see http://fr.wikipedia.org/wiki/Droit#La_loi_et_le_droit; www.stephane.info/show.php%3Fcode%3Dweblog&direct %3D641&lg%3Dfr.

12. Republic of Mali, 2006.
13. The International Day of Zero Tolerance to Female Genital Mutilation is celebrated on 6 February every year, following a UN appeal.
14. 'We have to be strict in order to put a stop to this practice' (Salouka, 2008).
15. Judicialisation: the increasingly systematic use of the courts to deal with difficult issues which earlier were always addressed out of court (Collectif Litec, 2007).
16. Unlike other contexts around the world (Butler, 2005).
17. The patriarchal system governs gender social relations, leading the masculine gender into a collectively and unconsciously assumed universalism.
18. After a number of terminological proposals (elderly, older persons, adults) the youth of the ICT–FGM project agreed on the notion of seniority in referring to 'non-youth'.
19. http://fr.wikipedia.org/wiki/Totem_et_Tabou.
20. Including, with respect especially to the public sphere, in matrilineal societies: http://fr.wikipedia.org/wiki/Famille_matrilinéaire.
21. The research led to the recognition of the closeness of the concepts of citizenship (collective construction of the city, a concept marked by Greek and Western thought) and village-centred collective/community development, which is even more of a reality in the African regions covered by the project.
22. Postmodernity is plural, relative, inductive, critical, complex and contextual. It questions and examines, develops different types of knowledge dialogue (scientific, experiential, traditional, etc.), favours dialectics between theory and practice, and evaluation of situations with hindsight. Here, democracy has a different meaning than it does in modernity: that of *a negotiation for participation in the transformation of social realities* that are at issue. Postmodernity tries not to be confined to big explanatory and general narrative theories and is wary of universal values (Sauvé, 2000).
23. National, local, ethnic, international.
24. Virtue derives from the word *vir*, which also gives the words 'virile', 'virility', 'virilism'. Whereas *vir* refers to a human being of the masculine gender, *virtus* denotes to virile strength and, by extension, *value*.
25. As well as the right to money and the right to the law (Marquès-Pereira, 2003).
26. That is, focused or centred on men.
27. In Senegal, for example (source: Sonatel phone company).
28. That is, both anti-citizenship and non-citizenship.
29. Experience reported in ENDA, 2007–08.

CHAPTER 3

1. The main results can be freely downloaded from the project website: www.famafrique.org/tic-mgf/accueil.html.
2. That is, community access to the Internet and mobile telephone network coverage.
3. Source: http://fr.wikipedia.org/.
4. *Nietàa*: 'evolution' in Bambara.
5. *Musso Dambe*: 'dignity of women' in Dioula.
6. The symposium 'FGM: The Citizenship Use of ICTs by Youth' (April–May 2008) was the culmination of the research process implemented as part of the ICT–FGM project. Its objective was to place youth, organised in associations, as direct beneficiaries of the project, in the centre of the action research issue and process on the citizenship contribution of ICTs to the abandonment of FGM, and especially to broaden the results of the conceptual, operational and community research obtained during the previous phases of the project: to build operationally the capacities and knowledge of youth and their associations; to promote many forms of mechanism and partnerships to ensure the sustainability of action plans, associations and the research project; to make progress in developing and launching the community action plans of youth associations.
7. Physical (physical presence) as opposed to virtual (online activity).
8. Including in the dialectical relation between the observed and the observer.
9. The unexpected debate with the 'traditionalists' was one example.
10. Girls are more sensitive to (i) private suffering, (ii) commonly mentioned risks (health, violence, violation of rights). Young men (i) show solidarity with girls and are personally sensitive to the sexual consequences for girls, and (ii) are personally concerned in their status as men (father, brother, parent).
11. For example, when they discussed the idea of providing spray paints for painting on the walls at the time of the symposium, because the youth were said to be good at expressing themselves in graffiti.
12. Only one personal experience was presented in public, drawing a great deal of sympathy from all the listeners.
13. In traditional cultures, and in francophone West Africa in particular, shame 'is the reverse of the moral code of a community', 'where there is an overpowering fear of public opinion and the torment of a guilt that rebounds on the whole community. The higher one's status in society, the greater one's sense of honour, and, therefore, of shame'; 'shame guarantees the perpetuity of traditional structures. In the Yatenga Mossi tribe, it serves to prevent the subjects of matrimonial exchange and

reproduction from deciding such matters: these processes, which are likely to be disrupted by any command over the secrecy of love affairs, must remain under the control of the elders'; 'Shame that victims find very difficult to escape from ..., overwhelmed as they are by the guilt of participating by force and betrayed by their own bodies' (Anselmini, 2004).

14. Gender relations, origin, race and social class are often mentioned, but few studies, by gender specialists or in Africa, have been devoted to gender relations and youth. Yet the transition to the information society, due to the spread of ICTs, suggests a real and specific generation gap. Exploring the transversality and interdependence of the two concepts, their organic relations to economics, power and culture, could shed light on a number of visions, policies and strategies in human life and the transformation of social relations.

15. The research found that youth are convinced about the relevance of ICTs in promoting the abandonment of FGM.


CHAPTER 4

1. Because FGM is not a divine requirement, and no revealed religion makes it obligatory (see, in particular, El Azar University, 2006).

2. As well as in other circumstances, such as rape during a war.

3. That is, second rate, a sort of 'variant' within a standard presumed to be universal (neutral), when actually its reference is the dominant male gender.

4. See Chapter 2 note 21.

5. That is, not only the right to physical integrity, protection against violence, and health, but also the right to pleasure and freedom.

6. In particular: respecting the rights of others, which are the same as their own; participating in the public affairs of the community.

7. For example, between the 'learned', those who know, and the 'ignorant', those who do not know.

8. Better separating women's affairs from men's affairs, for example.

9. Those who deny youths their citizenship capacity, for example.

10. I.e. top-down.

11. Which claims that in both the North and the South everybody – women, men and youth – are the same.

12. Those mentioned during the project are: illiteracy, diversity of African languages, low associational capacities, penetration, ICT access and accessibility.

CHAPTER 5

1. For example, the two editions of the 'Stop FGM Holidays' competition (2007 and 2008), in Bobo Dioulasso, which inspired the West African 'FGM: play and win' competition organised on the Lesjeuneschangent-lafrique.org Web site, in order to disseminate the results of the project among the public at large; and the Tostan digital literacy project for women, 'SMS Texting'.

2. It would be impossible to do this if FGM were considered simply 'women's business'.

3. The notion of privacy presupposes the human being/person and implies an entitlement to one's own separate private space, which should be respected and protected: a certain part of a person's life can remain confidential, belonging only to that person, being subject only to his/her personal choices, which do not have to be known or communicated to anybody outside of that private sphere.

4. The double bind refers to two opposing constraints (explicit or implicit): the obligation of each containing a prohibition of the other, which at first sight makes the situation impossible to resolve. Dual personality (schizophrenia) is both a defence mechanism for dealing with an impossible situation, and a final means of maintaining the cohesion of the group by trying to come to terms with the incoherence of the context (http://fr.wikipedia.org/wiki/Double_contrainte).

5. Especially joking relations, but also 'battle' (a rap scenario where groups challenge each other with 'no holds barred').

6. For example, the case of a girl born to a couple that is 'mixed' with respect to the practice of FGM: the mother belonging to an ethnic group that does not practise FGM accepting, against her will, her daughter being circumcised as a tribute (guarantee) to her FGM-practising in-laws. The girl knows that, within the setting provided by the project, she can count on a perception of her condition as a circumcised person that is different from that of her father's family.

7. Virilism: exacerbation of attitudes, representations and virile practices.

8. That is, in keeping with the education received in school and what they believed the project expected from them.

9. Lack in terms not of presence but of content.

CHAPTER 6

1. A nickname used by the youth during the symposium to make fun of their peers who underwent the technical training in blog creation.
2. Transformation of the modalities of social relations through their media representation within ICTs.
3. Which may be described in terms of 'progress', 'development', 'ethics' or 'wisdom'.

# References

AFARD/AAWORD (Association des Femmes Africaines pour la Recherche et le Développement) (1983) 'A Statement on Genital Mutilation', in Miranda Davies (ed.), *Third World: Second Sex, Women's Struggles and National Liberation*, London: Zed Books, 1983, p. 217, in http://aflit.arts.uwa.edu.au/MGF4.html.

Al Azhar University (2006) 'Conférence mondiale des ulémas sur l'interdiction de la violation du corps de la femme', 22–23 November 2006), www.famafrique.org/tic-mgf/DeclaratAl-AzharMGFNov06fr.doc.

Al Azhar University (2008) 'Égypte – Al-Azhar rejette un projet de loi visant à criminaliser l'excision', www.thememriblog.org/blog_personal/en/5997.htm.

d'Almeida-Topor, Hélène, Coquery-Vidrovitch, C., Goerg, O., and Guitart, F. (1992) *Les jeunes en Afrique*, Volume 1: *Evolution et rôle*; Volume 2: *La politique et la ville*, Paris: l'Harmattan, 1992.

Anselmini, Julie (2004) 'Anatomie de la honte', *Sigilia*, www.fabula.org/revue/document875.php.

Assogba, Yao (2007) *Regard sur la jeunesse en Afrique subsaharienne*, Quebec: Presses de l'Université Laval, www.pulaval.com/catalogue/regard-sur-jeunesse-afrique-subsaharienne-8987.html.

Baillette, Frédéric, and Liotard, Philippe, et al. (1999) *Sport et virilisme*, Montpellier: Éditions Quasimodo, www.revue-quasimodo.org/PDFs/SV2-SportVirilismeIntro.pdf.

Ballmer-Cao, Thanh-Huyen, et al. (2000) *Genre et politique, débats et perspectives*, Paris: Gallimard Folio.

Bissot, Hugues, and Mercier, Francine (n.d.) 'Excision et droit d'asile', www.dhdi.free.fr/recherches/etudesdiverses/articles/bissotmercier.htm.

Bourdieu, Pierre, and Passeron, Jean-Claude (1970) *La reproduction. Eléments pour une théorie du système d'enseignement*, Paris: Éditions de Minuit, www.unige.ch/fapse/life/livres/alpha/B/Bourdieu_Passeron_1970_A.html.

Butler, Judith (2005) *Trouble dans le genre. Pour un féminisme de la subversion*, Paris: La Découverte.

Camara, Sory (1992) *Gens de la parole: essai sur la condition et le rôle des griots dans la société malinké*, Paris: Karthala.

Collectif Litec (2007) *La société au risque de la judiciarisation*, Paris: Juris Classeur (LexisNexis), www.eyrolles.com/Droit/Livre/la-societe-au-risque-de-la-judiciarisation-9782711010196.

Deleuze, Gilles (1986) *Foucault*, Paris: Éditions de Minuit.

Deleuze, Gilles, and Guattari, Félix (1991) *Qu'est ce que la philosophie?* Paris: Éditions de Minuit.

Demers, Yannick (2003) 'Les hommes et le féminisme: intégrer la pensée féministe', http://sisyphe.org/spip.php?article695.

Dorlin, Elsa (2008) *Sexe, genre et sexualités*, Paris: PUF.

ENDA (2004) *Citoyennes africaines de la société de l'information*, Dakar, www.famafrique.org/regentic/e-citoyennes.pdf.

ENDA (2005) *Fracture numérique de genre en Afrique francophone: une inquiétante réalité*, Dakar, www.famafrique.org/regentic/indifract/fracturenumer-iquedegenre.pdf.

ENDA (2007a) *Rapport de l'analyse documentaire des documents publiés en ligne*, Dakar, Projet TIC-MGF, www.famafrique.org/tic-mgf/Rapport-FinalAnalyseDocumentaireProjetMGF-TIC.pdf.

ENDA (2007b) *Rapport de recherche de terrain au Sénégal*, Projet TIC-MGF, Dakar, www.famafrique.org/tic-mgf/espaceprive/RaprechSN.pdf.

ENDA (2007c) *Rapport de recherche de terrain au Mali*, Projet TIC-MGF, Dakar, www.famafrique.org/tic-mgf/espaceprive/RaprechML.pdf.

ENDA (2007d) *Rapport de recherche de terrain au Burkina-Faso*, Projet TIC-MGF, Dakar, www.famafrique.org/tic-mgf/espaceprive/RaprechBF.pdf.

ENDA (2007e) *Rapport final de l'Atelier méthodologique*, Projet TIC-MGFDakar, www.famafrique.org/tic-mgf/espaceprive/Rapport atelier method-ologique.pdf.

ENDA (2007–2008) *TIC&MGF, jeunes et citoyenneté en Afrique*, Forum virtuel MGF-TIC, www.famafrique.org/tic-mgf/introsforum.html.

ENDA (2008a) *TIC&MGF, jeunes et citoyenneté en Afrique' (juin 2007 – février 2008)*, Projet TIC-MGF Rapport d'évaluation du forum virtuel MGF-TIC, Dakar, www.famafrique.org/tic-mgf/EvaluationForumVirtuelM-GF-TIC.pdf.

ENDA (2008b) *Analyse critique de la Revue par les paires*, Projet TIC-MGF, Dakar, www.famafrique.org/tic-mgf/analysecritiqueRDP.pdf.

ENDA (2008c) *L'excision sur les murs*, Projet TIC-MGF, Dakar, www.fam-afrique.org/tic-mgf/SymposiumL'excisionSurLesMurs.pdf.

ENDA (2008d) *Regards croisés sur l'excision à l'heure des TIC, Jeunes et genre, au cœur de la citoyenneté*, Rapport d'évaluation du projet TIC-MGF, Dakar, www.famafrique.org/tic-mgf/ENDA-TIC-MGF-RapportEvaluation.pdf.

ENDA (2008e) 'EvalTIC-MGF', Groupe de discussion Evaluation, Projet TIC-MGF, http://fr.groups.yahoo.com/group/evalTIC-MGF/.

ENDA (2008f) 'Chercheures TIC-MGF', Projet TIC-MGF, http://groups.
google.sn/group/chercheures?hl=fr.

ENDA (2008g) 'EvalTIC-MGF' et Groupe de discussion Evaluation, Projet
TIC-MGF, http://fr.groups.yahoo.com/group/evalTIC-MGF/.

ENDA (2008h) Liste Equipes TIC-MGF, Projet TIC-MGF, http://groups.
google.sn/group/equipesTIC-MGF?hl=fr.

Enquêtes démographiques et de santé (Demographic and Health Surveys),
www.measuredhs.com/.

Eveno, E., Gueye, C., Guibbert J.-J., Oillo, D., and Sagna, O. (2008) Introduction in 'Sociétés africaines de l'information: illustrations sénégalaises',
*Netcom*, vol. 22, no. 1–2; and *Netsuds*, vol. 3.

Gaudet, Stéphanie (2007) 'L'émergence de l'âge adulte, une nouvelle étape
du parcours de vie; Implications pour le développement de politiques',
www.policyresearch.gc.ca/doclib/DP_YOUTh_Gaudet_200712_f.pdf.

Giraud, Pierre-Noël (2008) *La mondialisation, émergences et fragmentations*, Sciences Humaines Éditions.

Grawith, Madeleine (2001) *Méthodes des sciences sociales*, Paris: Dalloz.

Hirata, Helena, Laborie, Françise, Le Doare, Hélène, and Senotier, Danièle
(2000) *Dictionnaire critique du féminisme*, Paris: PUF.

Kaplan, Daniel (2005) 'Internet et innovation: Place de l'innovation dans la
société de l'information', www.internetactu.net/2005/06/23/internet-et-
innovation-place-de-linnovation-dans-la-socit-de-linformation/.

Marques-Pereira, Bérengère (2003) *La citoyenneté politique des femmes*, Paris: A.
Colin.

Morel Cinq-Mars, José (2002) *Quand la pudeur prend corps*, Paris: PUF.

Naji, J.E. (n.d.) 'L'appui et les limites de l'IEC aux campagnes de développement dans les pays du sud / Illustrations par le cas de la santé', www.sante.
gov.ma/smsm/santecomun/appuilimites.htm.

Ndiaye, Raphaël (1992) 'Correspondances ethno-patronymiques et parenté
plaisantante: une problématique d'intégration à large échelle', *Environnement africain*, vol. 8, no. 31–32 , 3–4 ENDA, Dakar,

No Peace Without Justice (2008) 'Déclaration du Caire Plus Cinq: Mettre
fin aux MGF par une mise hors la loi définitive: un objectif que nous
pouvons atteindre', www.npwj.org/_resources/_documents/Uploaded-
Files//Déclaration_Finale_Caire+5.pdf.

Organisation Internationale de la Francophonie (n.d.) 'Egalité des sexes et
développement – concepts et terminologie', http://genre.francophonie.
org/IMG/pdf/Egalite_des_sexes_et_developpement_-_concepts_et_ter-
minologie.pdf.

Ortigues, Edmond, and Marie-Cécile (1984) *Œdipe africain*, Paris:
L'Harmattan.

Population Council, 'Female genital cutting, Publications/resources', CD-Rom.

Population Reference Bureau (2001) (Liz Creel) 'Abandonner l'excision féminine: Prévalence, attitudes et efforts pour y mettre fin', www.measuredhs.com/gender/fgc-cd/pdfs/AbandoningFGC_Fr.pdf.

Population Reference Bureau (2005) 'Abandonner la mutilation génitale féminine/excision', CD-Rom.

Protocole à la Charte Africaine des Droits de l'homme et des Peuples Relatif aux Droits des Femmes www.africa-union.org/Official_documents/Treaties_Conventions_fr/Protocole_sur_le_droit_de_la_femme.pdf.

Quelques règles... pour rendre un texte épicène: www.univ-lyon1.fr/servlet/com.univ.collaboratif.utils.LectureFichiergw?CODE_FICHIER=121 4250703552&ID_FICHE=91775.

République du Mali (2006) *Programme National de Lutte contre la Pratique de l'Excision: Rapport général de la Conférence Sous-régionale Les Mutilations Génitales Féminines et la mise en Place du Protocole de Maputo'*, Bamako, Mali, 21–22 February, www.pnle-mali.org/IMG/pdf/rapport2006.pdf.

République du Sénégal (2008) Ministère de la Famille, de la Solidarité Nationale et de l'Entreprenariat Féminin et de la Micro Finance (2008) *Atelier régional pour l'abandon de l'excision/ mutilation génitale féminine*, Rapport de synthèse, Dakar, Senegal, 13 October.

Salouka, P. Boureima (2008) 'Le Burkina déclare la Tolérance Zéro contre la pratique de l'excision', http://criged.org/index. php?view=article&catid=29:genre-jeunesse-sexualite&id=52: tolerance-zero&tmpl=component&print=1&page=.

Sauvé, Lucie (2000) 'L'éducation relative à l'environnement entre modernité et postmodernité Les propositions du développement durable et de l'avenir viable', www.unites.uqam.ca/ERE-UQAM/membres/articles/ERE4.pdf.

Sembene, Ousmane (2005) *Moolaadé*, film.

Shaaban, Layla M., and Harbiso, Sarah (2005) 'Reaching the Tipping Point against Female Genital Mutilation', *The Lancet*, www.popcouncil.org/pdfs/frontiers/journals/lancet_fgc2005.pdf.

Sulami, Abdel Rahman (2001) *La courtoisie en Islam*, Paris: Iqra.

Thiam, Awa (1978) *La parole aux négresses*, Paris: Denoel–Gonthier.

Tourné, Karine (2001) 'Le chômeur et le prétendant, Les maux de la jeunesse ou l'impossible passage à l'âge adulte', *Égypte/Monde arabe*, http://ema.revues.org/index876.html.

UNICEF (2005a) *Female Genital Mutilation/Cutting: A Statistical Exploration*, www.unicef.org/french/publications/files/FGM-C_final_10_October.pdf.

UNICEF (2005b) *Changer une convention sociale néfaste: la pratique de l'excision/ mutilation génitale féminine*, Centre de recherche Innocenti, www.unicef-irc.org/publications/pdf/fgm_fr.pdf.
UNICEF (2008) *Evaluation à long terme du programme de Tostan au Sénégal: régions de Kolda, Thiès et Fatick*, www.childinfo.org/files/fgmc_tostan_fr.pdf.
Union interparlementaire (2002) 'Législation et autres textes de droit interne', Campagne parlementaire 'halte a la violence contre les femmes, les mutilations sexuelles féminines', www.ipu.org/wmn-f/fgm-prov.htm.

## Websites

AIDOS: www.aidos.it.
Association Musso Dambe: www.associationmoussodambe-bf.cabanova.fr.
ENDA: www.enda.sn.
Famafrique: www.famafrique.org.
GEEP: www.geep.org.
GTZ: www.gtz.de.
IAC: http://iac-ciaf.com.
ICT–FGM: www.famafrique.org/tic-mgf/accueil.html.
ICT–FGM, Citizenship portal on FGM: www.ticetmgf.fr.gd.
ICRD: www.idrc.ca.
Intact: www.intact-network.net.
Jeunes de Ségou en avant–Niètaa: www.nietaassociation.fr.gd.
Population Council: www.popcouncil.org.
Population Reference Bureau: www.prb.org.
Programme National de Lutte contre l'Excision (Mali): www.pnle-mali.org.
Secrétariat Permanent du Comité de Lutte contre l'Excision (Burkina-Faso): www.sp-cnlpe.gov.bf.
Stopfgmc: www.stopfgmc.org.
The Youth Are Changing Africa: www.lesjeuneschangentlafrique.org.
Tostan: www.tostan.org.
UNICEF: www.unicef.org.

# Index

# African Sexualities: A Reader

## Sylvia Tamale

2011
paperback £24.95
978-0-85749-016-2

*African Sexualities* inspires readers to study, reflect and gain insights from African perspectives into the complex issues of gender and sexuality in an African context. The authors of this groundbreaking book provide a critical mapping of the plurality of African sexualities while also challenging the reader to question assumptions.

Incorporating original research and analysis, life stories and artistic expression, this accessible but scholarly book examines dominant and deviant sexualities, analyses the body as a site of political, cultural and social contestation and investigates the intersections between sex, power, masculinities and femininities. The feminist approach analyses sexuality within various structures of oppression – patriarchal, capitalist, colonial, neocolonial – while also highlighting its emancipatory potential.